Terceira
The Lilac Island

Terceira
The Lilac Island

A History and Guide to Terceira Island
of the Azores Archipelago

Allan Rodney Tilley

Amazon KDP Publishing USA

A Self-Published Book by Allan Rodney Tilley

Copyright 2021 by Allan Rodney Tilley

ISBN # 9798419416512

45 Wildwood Lane

Kerrville, Texas 78028 USA

Email: randjtilley@yahoo.com

Cover photo by permission from Sarah Tilley

Edits by Judy Tilley and Esther Tilley

Formatting by Aslamkhan116

Dedication

This book is dedicated to all the friendly people who call Terceira home. They have shown through their lives love for faith, family, and friends. They have preserved one of the most beautiful islands in the world: Terceira. I thank you for sharing your island with us.

Table of Contents

Chapter One: Physical Geography 1
Chapter Two: History of Terceira 10
Chapter Three: Tourism in Terceira 38
Chapter Four: Traditional Food of Terceira 73
Chapter Five: Flora and Fauna 78
Chapter Six: People and Culture 84
Chapter Seven: Art and Architecture 91
Chapter Eight: Practical Tips for Tourists 94
Chapter Nine: Facts and Figures 96
Chapter Ten: Terceira Trivia 98
Attributions 100
Additional Books by Allan Rodney Tilley 102

Chapter One
Physical Geography:

I slands have always carried with them a mystic of the unknown and a fantasy of lands, long forgotten, in faraway unexplored corners of the ocean. Whenever you hear of a shipwreck, it is always a story of someone marooned on a deserted tropical island with wild lions, elephants, and tigers. When you watch movies of lost lands and subtropical destinations where dinosaurs roam, it is always on an island. Islands have always carried an intrigue, a mystery, an untold story of times past, and the island of Terceira fits all of those preconceived ideas, for, in the island's history, dreams of utopia were formulated. Terceira Island is one of the most beautiful islands of the nine islands that make up the Azores Archipelago, and for many of those who first landed on these shores, paradise was found.

It is an island that pushes its way from the depths of the ocean to rise in a rainbow of colors. It is known as the *"Lilac or Violet Island"* because of its beautiful flowers that line every road, field, and mountain crevice. The people of Terceira love their flowers and it is not uncommon to see front yards filled with flowerpots overrun with a variety of greenery. Street posts in every major city have hanging baskets of flowers flowing down onto the streets, and since Terceira is a subtropical climate, flowers thrive without much care needed. When tourists experience the island for the first time, most are overwhelmed by the massive amount of flowers present; especially the blue and lilac hydrangeas. However, more than the mountains of flowers are the variation of green hues that blanket the mountains and fields. Offset that with black volcanic rock walls that crisscross the island, along with grazing black and white dairy cows and clear blue seas with white foam from the breaking of waves, and you have a virtual paradise. Many make the comparison with other tropical islands and have nicknamed Terceira: *"The Hawaii of the Atlantic."* Whether in summer or winter, the temperature is moderate with the average temperature staying within a 30-degree variation.

   Terceira is the third island of the Azores to be discovered by the Portuguese in 1437, and it is from this fact that the island derives its name; "Terceira," meaning third in English. Terceira Island was first called the *"Island of Jesus Christ"* by the Portuguese sailors since it was discovered on the first day of January, which is the feast day of the name of Jesus, and also because the discovery was made by a Portuguese sea captain who was in the *"Order of Christ."* However, the name of the island remained only temporarily, and it soon was changed to "Terceira" as it was the third island in the nine-island Azores archipelago. The Azores sit in the middle of the North Atlantic Ocean, 1408 kilometers (875 miles) from Portugal, and 3958 kilometers (2460 miles) from New York. Air travel is only a four-hour direct flight from Boston, Massachusetts, and a two-hour flight from Lisbon, Portugal. There are also numerous airline links to the European mainland as well. Terceira is one of the larger islands of the archipelago with an area of 400.28km2 (154.55 square miles). It has a population of 56,000, which makes it second only to the island of San Miquel in population density. Terceira is a part of a chain of mountains that run along the Mid-Atlantic Ridge that separates the Eurasian and African plates to the east, and the South and North American plates to the west.[1] The other islands along this ridge are Iceland, Bermuda, Ascension, Tristan da Cunha, and of course, the Azores Islands.

All of the nine islands were created when magma pushed through the cracks and fractures in the earth's crust and erupted as volcanoes arising off of the ocean floor to become what today is known as the Azores. Geologists still consider the Azores to be an active zone of volcanic concern as tremors, eruptions, and volcanic activity are still notable. For example, in 1957, there was the eruption of the Capelinhos Volcano on Faial Island on September 27th of that year. The island had to be evacuated with much of its population resettling in America. The island is still in the process of rebuilding and recovery. Terceira has areas of volcanic activity as well. Some of these volcanic areas still spew out sulfuric gas daily and are off-limits to tourists. However, the island of Terceira has remained geologically stable and there appears to be no danger from any extreme volcanic activity of any sort at this time. The volcanic craters, caves, calderas, fissures, and crevices that make up the three hundred known cavities of volcanic origin seen today have been dormant for eons of time. They remain only as a tourist attraction and a source of rich volcanic soil lending to the agricultural heritage that makes the island a paradise to behold.

---

[1] Direcao Regional de Turismo dos Acores, (2018). *Terceira Mapa Turistico*, Horta, Faial, Azores, Portugal.

Geologically, Terceira is around a million years old, as well as the islands of Faial, Graciosa, and Sao Jorge. Pico Island is the youngest island of the Azores having been created around 300,000 years ago. The Azores continue to amaze scientists and geologists alike with new geological phenomenal appearing and disappearing. As late as 1811, a new island appeared east of San Miquel, only to last four months until the sea swallowed it again. The island remained exposed long enough to be claimed by the British and given the name, "Sabrina," but was soon lost to the violent elements of nature, never to return, thereby taking the British flag along with it and the name. [2]

Terceira, although not the largest island, has been the place of legends and political intrigue, with tales of fallen kings, and lost explorers. It is not a coral island as many islands are in the Atlantic, but it is an island of fire and ice, having endured the lingering ice age ravages, as well as the volcanic eruptions that still today define the island's character. It is neither an island of sand with the erosion of limestone, nor is it an island of sedimentary organic materials, but it is an island formed from violent magma upheavals found in the imagination of science fiction writers and amateur archeologists. It is an island that stirs up emotions of the unknown past and fantasies of future aspirations.

---

[2] Azores History. (2019). *Geological History of the Azores*. Retrieved 1/7/22 from http://landenweb.com/azores/history/

Today, as one views the pristine landscapes and the pastoral settings with lazy dairy cows grazing in the sun, it is hard to imagine that at one time this island would have been hellish. It would have been shaken by violent eruptions, earthquakes, and clouds of mist and dust. It would be an island that held new plant species never seen before and animal life that survived only by learning to adapt to black ash and volcanic tuff. Nature took its toll, but the island lived on, and today we are witnesses to the past and varied life of this island we call Terceira.

On Terceira, the largest and oldest volcanic complex is the Cinco Picos Volcanic Complex (Serra do Cume) which was active around 375,000 years ago. After its collapse, it left an enormous "caldera" or crater seven by nine kilometers (four by six miles) in diameter. The deposit of pumice and the resulting cinder flow left an uninterrupted plain of fertile lands which today sustains the many black and white dairy cows that come to characterize the island and its distinctive logo. The youngest stratovolcano is the dormant Santa Barbara volcano which forms the highest summit on the island at 1021 meters.

However, the most important and highly visible area of volcanic activity on the island is the basaltic lava flow that left the pumice cone known today as Monte Brasil. Monte Brasil (Mount Brazil) defines the harbor for the city of Angra do Heroismo, providing a protective shelter for the anchoring of ships and yachts. The imposing Spanish fortifications of a bygone era, which can still be seen today, make ample use of the natural defenses, as it again utilizes the tuff cone for military defenses. It rises to a height of 205 meters (673 feet) with a diameter of one kilometer (0.62 miles). The name *"Mount Brazil"* is said to be taken from the brazilwood tree, which was an important commodity in the making of woolen dyes, while others speculate that the name is derived from the island that was mentioned in early Irish legends connected with St. Brendon. According to the legend, the island was supposed to be covered in fog and seen once every seven years. As said earlier, this idea is what island myths are made from.[3]

If you take the legend of St. Brendon, and couple both Terceira and Ireland, and the similarities of the rock walls that crisscross both countries, you will think that the legend of St. Brendon does appear to have a rational conclusion. The black lava walls of Terceira's pastures were a natural resource, as the early settlers sought to tame the wild island that abounded with thick forests and brush. They

---

[3] Perfect Tourist. (2015). *Terceira Island: History*. Retrieved 1/7/22 from www.azores.theperfecttourist.com.

would first slash and burn the forests and then turn the goats out to defoliate the greenery. It would create new patches of land for agriculture, but the rocks remained as a constant reminder of the wilderness that still existed. Gradually, and with much labor, the early colonialists, with pick and hoe, would lift the stones, skid them into place, and begin the construction of a wall that would divide and conquer the land. Today, as in Ireland, walls are a constant reminder of man over nature. If today, St. Brendon were to visit Terceira he would be sure that his native Irelanders had expanded their reach to the mid-Atlantic and beyond. E. Estyn Evans, the Irish folklorist wrote, *"The history of rural Ireland could be read out of doors, had we the skills, from the scrawling made by men in the field boundaries of successive periods."* [4] That could be rightly said of Terceira as well, as you feel the personality of the islanders, as they sought to change Terceira from a wild island swept by foreboding winds to an island of touristic beauty and agriculture sustainability. The volcanic activity of times past has been a god-sent blessing, for now, the island has all the factors necessary for an enjoyable life: sea and sun, mountains and valleys, and fresh fruit and vegetables. What more could you want?

However, it is not always rosy and volcanic tremors in the year 2022 was again active in the neighboring islands causing many to be alarmed as to the future of the islands. Neighboring Saint George Island had to be evacuated and the island was put on high alert for the possibility of a new volcanic eruption. Every island of the Azores has experienced tremors in recent years, although mild in nature, it still represents a reason to be cautious when you travel and visit the islands.

---

[4] MacWeeney, A., and Conniff, R., *The Stone Walls of Ireland.* (1986). London: Thames and Hudson, Ltd.

Sulfuric Gases at a Volcanic Fissure

Earthquakes are also a major concern for Terceira as well, with many seismic events produced by the Lajes and Fontinhas faults that run underneath the island. On January 1, 1980, a large earthquake hit Angra do Heroismo, and major damage was incurred to the downtown historic district. The town was rebuilt and was declared a UNESCO World Heritage Site in 1983. But today smaller earthquakes are still frequently felt throughout the island, but with no considerable damage to be seen. The island is constantly being monitored for any seismic activity and an early warning system is coordinated through the forty seismic stations placed throughout the islands.

Now and in times past, the majority of the islanders live in a ring along the sea's edge that encircles the island. Some say that the residential centers are situated thusly because of the fear of volcanic eruptions, which would leave only the sea into which to flee, while others say that people live near the sea because of the nature of the fishing industry and the identity of seafaring ancestry. No matter what, the nature of volcanic island life continues to define the people of Terceira. As for the tourists, it makes a great story to tell friends back home and it makes for some fantastic photography.[5] If you think of the Azores as comparable to Hawaii you will not be alarmed as to the nature of the volcanic activity. Hawaii and its vast lava flows have been turned into a tourist destination instead of a area of extreme caution and I assume Terceira could do the same.

---

[5] Varela, R., (Ed). (2003). *Acores*. Rio de Mouro, Portugal: Everest Editora

Chapter Two
History of Terceira:

Megalithic History

Grota do Medo Tombs

When Terceira Island was discovered by the Portuguese in 1437 by Goncalo Velho Cabral, there was no indication that the island had ever been inhabited. When the Portuguese arrived, the islands were empty of all human and animal life except for birds and insects, and a few small mammals, such as mice and bats. There were no remains of any settlement of any kind. The Portuguese assumed that they were the first to step foot on Terceira, and rightly so. However, in recent years, scholars, scientists, and archaeologists have made some surprising pre-Portuguese discoveries that appear to put the colonizing of the island back to the Bronze Age and maybe even earlier. Although Terceira's history is shrouded in controversy, new discoveries, as always, push our imagination and our thinking to take new roads in academic research.

In a previously unexplored region of Grota do Medo (Posto Santo), (not a tourist attraction as of now), evidence was found of a megalithic structure that could date back to the Neolithic period of prehistory. Researchers and archaeologists have found what appears to be a passage grave or tomb built in a similar fashion to those found throughout Europe. Throughout England and Scotland, similar tombs also exist. They are classified into four distinct types: court tombs, passage tombs, portal tombs, and wedge tombs.[6] There

---

[6] Manning, C., *Irish Field Monuments*. (1985). Dublin, Commissioners of Public

are two tombs identified so far on Terceira. The first one is a type of passage grave that extends back into the mound for about 4m and then opens up into a burial chamber, which is circular and about 3m in diameter. The other tomb on top of the first tomb, but not unlike the first, is larger, being 7.5m long and 4.5m in diameter. If they are indeed passage tombs, then they would date back to between 4000 to 2000 BC.

They are constructed on a high point in the island's landscape in the proximity of Pico do Espigao. As of this time, no "official" archaeological excavations have been sanctioned and no additional artifacts have been found, such as pottery or statuaries.

However, additional evidence of earlier habitation continues to intrigue scholars and scientists alike as they find other stone examples of early Bronze Age evidence of human habitation. Near the passage graves over twenty carved bowls in the surrounding rocks were found, some circular in construction, while others have defined rectangular edges. There are also man-made engravings on some of the stones that resemble a type of early alphabet or rock art, along with "cup-marks" and "cut-marks" as well. As stated in the book, *A Guide to Ancient Sites in Britain* (1979), *"The subject of the cup and ring marks, as these carvings are often called, is a highly controversial one.... There have, of course, been many interpretations of the variety of symbols recorded (maps of ancient sites; sacrificial symbols, the cups holding blood; primitive sundials; a game; mortars for grinding grains, seeds, etc.; molds used in metal casting; adder lairs; knife-sharpeners; mason marks; lamps; writing...."*[7] Some of the stones in Terceira have more than one hundred such marks on a single large stone. Some marks have been drawn in a circular manner, while other inscriptions are semi-

---

Works. Pp. 13-14.
[7] Bord, J. and C., *A Guide to Ancient Sites in Britain*. (1979). London, Collins Publishing house, pp. 99.

circular. All of these discoveries can be readily seen and are not unlike other discoveries in Ireland, England, and Spain. You can see the exact same symbols seen in Terceira at the Lordenshaw Hillfort site and at the Roughting Linn Inscribed Stone, both in Northumberland, England.

As this is not an "official" tourist destination and preliminary findings are still being examined, outside tourism is not being encouraged as the local authorities and the academic community have not been able to make an adequate excavation of the site, therefore, the actual site is not open for amateur archaeological studies. The site is restricted to scholarly endeavors and vandalism is discouraged and feared lest an important "find" is destroyed, never to be replicated again. Additional discussion and photos can be seen in scholarly journals as listed on the internet. [8]

Furthermore, there are additional phenomena equally elusive in our understanding of early prehistory, such as the Serreta Ruins, and the "cart-ruts" of St. Bras and Porto Martins.

Serreta Ruins

Near the village of Serreta on the northwest side of the island, there are a series of ruins unlike any other ruins seen on the island. There is no historical data on record that documents the existence of these ruins in any archive in the city offices or governmental agencies. These walls and passages are spread over a large area in places not viable for agriculture and they are now covered with trees and dense underbrush. They are not of the construction as seen in the walls built throughout the island by the Portuguese, but as of yet, no one has identified what the walls are an indication of or for what

---

[8] Rodrigues, A., Martins, N., Ribeiro, N., Joaquinto, A., (2019) *Early Atlantic Navigation: Pre-Portuguese Presence in the Azores Islands.* Nova Scriptorium. Retrieved 1/1/22 from https://novoscriptorium.com.

purpose they were made. It is a large complex located in the area last settled in Terceira, and it remains a mystery as to the nature and purpose of this walled settlement. Some have suggested that the ruins are from the same time period as the other megalithic structures prevalent on the island, but as of yet no scholarly archaeological study has been done to verify that. They do appear to be similar to the walls and construction that are seen on the islands of Scotland and in Ireland.

Cart ruts of S. Bras and Porto Martins

On the northeast side of the island, there are many instances of cart ruts left in the rock surfaces, apparently made by ancient wagons or carts carrying heavy loads of materials. The first mention of the cart ruts was in 1859 by the historian, Francisco Ferreira Drummond. In interviews with the island's elders, he was told that the appearance of the ruts had been there for generations, and most felt that the ruts had preceded the Portuguese arrival on the islands in 1437. In 2015-2016, the City Hall of Angra do Heroismo had the vegetation removed that was growing over and inside the cart ruts, and began to examine the length and depth of the ruts to determine their possible origin. The ruts run for almost 300m+ and can be seen in the area of the Guilherme Moniz Volcano complex. The incisions are from 3cm to 40 cm in-depth, with the gauge or width of the cart tracks between 1.1m to 1.4m. There are additional cart ruts that run to the sea's edge as seen in the village of Porto Martins. No one knows of any mention of the cart-ruts builders in earlier records, but Charles Darwin on his assessment of Terceira's topography in 1836, while taking his round the world trip aboard the *"Beagle,"* mentions them and was told by the elders of Terceira that they were, *"The Passage of the Beasts."* Darwin stayed four days in Terceira for further study and investigation, and upon returning to England he authored his book, *"The Voyage of the Beagle."* In that book,

Darwin (1836) makes a correlation between the Terceira ruts with the cart ruts that he had seen in the ancient pavement in Pompeii, Italy, and he supposed that they had been made by the Romans during an earlier age in Pompeii. He assumed that the cart-ruts on the island of Terceira were of Roman origin as well. [9]

In contradiction, many scholars have indicated that they are similar to the cart ruts seen on the Island of Malta. The ruts in Malta run across the island and into the sea and appear to be similar in gauge and depth to those seen in Terceira. The assumption is that the cart ruts in Malta and the ruts seen on Terceira are from the Bronze Age or earlier and perhaps they were made by the same people group. In a further analysis of the ruts, during the removal of the rocks and vegetation covering the indentions, they were found to be also covered by volcanic ash. If that ash came from the eruption of Pico Alto, then the cart ruts would be at least a thousand years old. The mystery continues to elicit much debate among the archaeological community, and they are anxious for additional studies to be done on the cart-ruts of Terceira so that a more accurate date as to the colonization of the Azores can be formulated. Terceira Island, although small in size, will certainly yield major breakthroughs in our understanding of ancient history in the future.[10]

---

[9] Darwin, C. (1958). *The Voyage of the Beagle*. New York: Bantam Books
[10] Rodregues, F., Madruga, J., Martins, N. and Cardoso, F. (2018). Dating the Cart-Ruts of Terceira Island, Azores, Portugal. *Archaeological Discovery*, 6, 279-299, doi: 10.4236/ad.2018.64014 retrieved 1/10/22 from https://doi.org/10/4236/ad.2018.64014.

Cart-Ruts of S. Bras

Bronze Age History

Mount Brasil Hypogea or Sanctuaries

On the west peak of Mount Brazil (Monte Brasil) is Pico of the Zimbreiro, and it is where some scholars have found ancient cave structures that they believe are a collection of ancient "hypogeum" or as defined, "ancient structures carved into stone that was used as burials." These structures can also be referred to as catacombs and are usually subterranean, but in the case of Phoenician or Carthaginian burial sites, they are typically in a "high place," as referenced in the Old Testament in the Bible. The Phoenicians worshipped the goddess of the sea, Asherah, who was seen as a representative of the god of fertility and her symbol was a phallic symbol or pole. The worship centers are usually located on the slope or on the side of a mountain with a source of water nearby for ablutions or ritual cleansing ceremonies. Sometimes the "high places" were in the center of a grove of trees with a tall tree or standing pillar as the center for pagan idol worship. [11]

If this is the case, and the caves found on Mount Brazil and Forte de Sao Diogo are Phoenician burial sites, then they could possibly date back to the fourth century BC. According to APIA's archaeologist, Nuno Ribeiro, (2012) *"More than five hypogea type monuments (tombs excavated in rocks) and at least three 'sanctuaries' proto historic, carved into the rock were found."* [12] The caves are linked to conduits to collect fresh water for ritual cleansings or baths, and some appear to be fashioned for sacrificial offerings. Previously Greek and Carthaginian coins were also found on the island to fortify the theory that Terceira has a long history of human habitation before the Portuguese arrival in the 1400s. The caves also correspond to other such ritual sites as seen in the Middle East and throughout the Mediterranean World. When we include the caves with their ceremonial water cisterns, rock-cut "chairs," niches for idol placement, along with the triangular geometry of the caves, this appears to be a site that needs extensive academic study to confirm the analysis that would push Azorean history back thousands of years. Phoenicians are known to be sea-faring people, but to what extent, history only knows. Some have even suggested that the Phoenicians sailed to the Americas. and who knows, maybe their first stop was at the Island of Terceira.[13]

Additionally, some have stated that they have found Sunni Islamic inscriptions on the island and claim that if they are legitimate, they would predate the Portuguese as well. It is possible since many African Muslim slaves were channeled on their way to the Americas through the Azores by the Portuguese and other

---

[11] Tilley, A., (2018). *A History and Guide to Biblical Sites in Cyprus.* Columbia, SC., USA, CreateSpace.
[12] Matos, C., (2012). *Archaeology: Prehistoric rock art found in caves on Terceira Island- Azores, 2-4/8*, Retrieved on 1/10/22, from http://portuguese-american-journal.com
[13] Costa, A., (2012). *Terceira Island as a "megalithic station." Factual description of some archaeological materials.* retrieved on 1/10/22 from http://www.ancient-wisdom.co.uk/portoazores.htm.

European nations, inscriptions from Islamic sources could be a recent occurrence, and not as old as originally thought. According to Boxer (1973), the Portuguese secured over 150,000 slaves from Africa between the years 1450-1500. [14] These slaves were funneled through the islands of the Azores and Madeira and were sold all over the Americas. Some were sold to Italy and Spain as well. They worked the fields of wheat and sugar cane and became a part of the North American mosaic of people that would finally be divided among the English, French, Spanish, and Portuguese. Further investigation as to this one particular inscription will undoubtedly reveal the authenticity of the dating and the origin of these inscriptions, but as of now, the debate continues.

There can be no doubt that a megalithic history was present at one time on the island of Terceira, and it will remain a mystery and a conversation of controversy for years to come. Again, it is the "stuff" that legends are made of and a wonder that causes us to keep seeking and looking for the truth that is just under the surface of every unturned stone.

---

[14] Boxer., (1973). *The Portuguese Seaborne Empire 1415-1825*. Harmondsworth, Penguin Books.

Pre-Portuguese History

The City of Atlantis

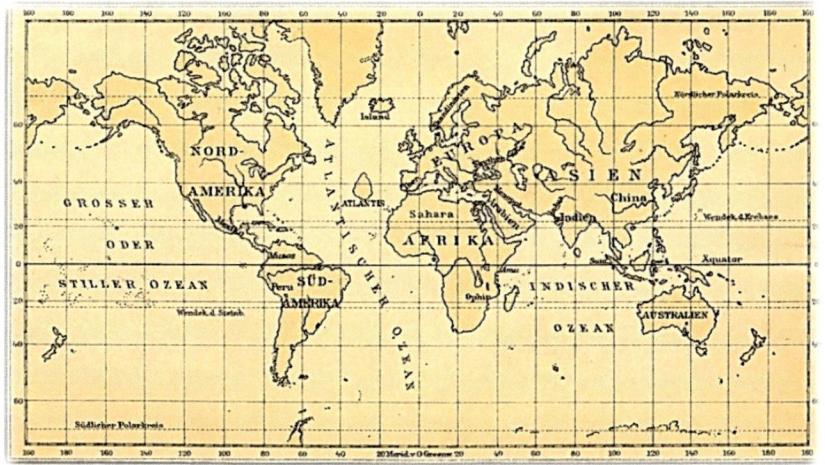

Early Map Showing Atlantis as the Azores

The theory of the mystical city of Atlantis has puzzled archaeologists, historians, and treasure hunters alike. Atlantis has been identified separately as the Island of Crete, the Canary Islands, the City of Cadiz, Spain, and of course the Azores. Since the Portuguese "discovered" the Azores in the 1400s, much speculation has been made as to the possibility that the Azorean islands are all that is left after the catastrophic volcanic eruption that destroyed the fabled utopia of Atlantis. Atlantis, also called Atalantis or Atlantica, has been sought, found, and lost again over ions of time. Supposedly, the island nation of advanced, peaceful people with 10,000 chariots, and untold wealth was arranged in a series of islands in a circular fashion somewhere in the Atlantic Ocean. It was located beyond the "Pillars of Hercules" which today we know as the Straights of Gibraltar. The Greek philosopher, Plato, in his two dialogues, *"Timaeus and Critias,"* written 2400 years ago, mentioned this fabled tale. Some say it was only a mystical parable to highlight Plato's ideology, while others feel that it was a story told orally for years and later written by Plato, years after the disastrous event.

For years, the story was seen only as Greek mythology, but with the publication of *"Atlantis: The Antediluvian World"* by Ignatius Donnelly in 1882, Atlantis fever would be reignited and the quest for this mystical city would emerge as a credible archaeological investigation. According to Donnelly (1882), *"The Azores Islands are undoubtedly the peaks of the mountains of Atlantis."*[15] He further indicates that Plato spoke of the hot and cold springs that dotted the island of Atlantis and Donnelly surmises that the numerous hot and cold springs that are in abundance in the Azores are indeed the same springs that were found on the Island of Atlantis. Throughout his book, Donnelly makes numerous references to the correlation between the tale of Atlantis and the Azores. He is convinced that only the Azores have the exact coordinates and the topography necessary to be recognized as the location of Atlantis.

James W. Mavor, Jr. in *"Voyage to Atlantis"* (1996) wrote, *"Modern scientists have narrowed the search down to two possibilities: the Atlantic either in the Azores or the Bahamas; and the Mediterranean, at Santorini or Crete."*[16] He also noted that one of the popular pastimes mentioned by Plato for the people of Atlantis was the capturing of wild bulls with ropes. The similarity to the wild "bullfights" of Terceira, which although similar in nature, would take a lot of imagination to correlate.

However, other scholars and historians such as Sir C. Wyville Thompson in his book, *"Voyage of the Challenger"* (1877) noted

---

[15] Donnelly, I. (1882). *Atlantis, the Antediluvian World.* New York: Gramercy Publishing Company.
[16] Mavor, J. (1996). *Voyage to Atlantis,* Aurora, Illinois: Inner Traditions International, LTD.

he large black lava walls on many islands of the Azores, including those of Terceira, would indicate a huge volcanic eruption occurred that could have destroyed any cities that may have been on the island, including Atlantis.[17]

Roman Ruins

In addition to all the other evidence of pre-history on the island, another piece of evidence could be the discovery of the columbarium (pigeon incubation chamber) that appears to be of Roman origin and can be found on Mount Brasil as well. It is impressive as to the size and construction in that it is built into solid rock, and although exposed to the elements, it is remarkably well preserved. It is of similar construction to columbariums found on the Canary Islands and the Iberian Peninsula.

Other mysterious prehistoric discoveries include a part of a Roman column found in Angra do Heroismo and a piece of pottery or ceramic found in a megalithic structure and dated to 2530 years ago. There are the standing stones, (similar to the Carnac Stones of France), which are found in some of the walls that separate the pastures on Terceira, and the most controversial find of all; the underwater "pyramid" found off the coast of Terceira.

Terceira Underwater Pyramid

In 2013 on a recreational boat trip, a fisherman by the name of Dioclesiano Silva was looking for a good fishing spot, when according to his GPS, he saw what he believed to be an underwater pyramid. Since this area of the sea has been covered with water for the past 20,000 years, this discovery, if it were true, would be a major milestone in the understanding of early human history. Silva

---

[17] Thompson, W. (1877) *Voyage of the Challenger: The Atlantic.* New York: Harper and Brothers

told the local paper, *Diaro Insular,* "The pyramid is perfectly shaped and oriented by the cardinal points." [18] Using today's GPS digital technology, the pyramid is said to be sixty meters tall with a base of eight thousand square meters and sits in forty meters of water off the coast of Terceira. If this is true, then the pyramid would certainly change the history of Terceira and its origins. The Portuguese Navy is presently studying the structure and as of now, no definitive report has been released. Until further study can be done, no conclusion can be drawn, and the mystery remains. [19]

Western European History of Terceira

Age of Discovery

In the Middle Ages, European nations were beginning their age of discovery. Not since the time of Marco Polo had there been such monumental discoveries as when the nations of Portugal, Spain, and England began to sail to the ends of the earth and beyond. They rounded the Horn of Africa, and the Cape, and India was discovered. They went beyond the Pillars of Hercules, which in earlier times was considered to be the limit of any landmass, only to discover the Americas and most of the islands in between. They went onto China, Japan, the Philippines, and throughout Africa and Asia, establishing trading stations and colonies until they came to control most of the world.

---

[18] Silva, D., (2012). Underwater Pyramid Discovered. *Diaro Insular Newspaper*
[19] Oonadivers. (2020). *Underwater Pyramid Discovered Near Portugal.* Retrieved 1/17/22 from http://www.oonasdivers.com.

1304 Portrait of Saint Brendan

The earliest European documentary record of what most assume to be the Azores Islands is the tradition linked to Saint Brendan of Ireland. St. Brendan was born in Ireland in 484AD and established several monasteries throughout Ireland and England. Tradition states that later, St. Brendan would go off to sea in search of the Garden of Eden or a paradise of sorts that he believed was to the west of Ireland. He traveled throughout the northern Atlantic and after passing through the "sea of darkness" he came upon what he called, "a marvelous island" which he assumed was the promised land that all saints would finally sail to. Many feel that he had discovered one of the islands of the Azores. The story or legend was so believable that many early cartographers included the Island of St. Brendan on their maps, albeit in various locations.

The Azores, until the Portuguese discovered and colonized them, were only hinted at by cartographers and historians. Nautical maps as early as 1325 suggested there were islands beyond Ireland and in a chart by Angelino Dalarto, an island west of Ireland was identified and he named it "Bracile". Later, Angelino Dulcert (1339) also identified other islands in the Atlantic and made mention of "Capraria" which most scholars assume is referencing the Azores. The Medici

Atlas, created in 1351 and recreated in 1370, again made mention of the Azores and included the seven of the nine islands that were known to exist. In light of this knowledge of cartography, it is well known that, although uninhabited, the Azores, including the Island of Terceira, was known to geographers and scholars alike.

The Azores were legendary at the time for they could be the answer to their quest by the Europeans for the Kingdom of the Seven Cities, The Fortunate Islands, The Island of Brasil, The Land of the Codfish, and as stated earlier, The Land of Atlantis. Treasure hunters, along with the monarchs of Europe, were eager to find these distant lands and then strip them of their gold and jewels, thereby strengthening their fortunes and treasure reserves. Everyone, from the Muslim pirates of the Mediterranean to the explorers of Portugal and Spain, all were eager to hear a delightful story and to follow that tradition or legend to the ends of the earth. In 1436, the island we know presently as Terceira was placed on the map by the cartographer, Andrea Biano, and named, *"The Island of Brasil."* It is a name that has come to be identified to this day with Terceira with the naming of the volcanic cone that sits at the edge of the harbor of Angra do Heroismo, *"The Mount of Brasil."*

As far as the "official" discovery of Terceira is concerned, various accounts as to whom, what, when, and where are still under discussion. In 1427, the first island of the Azores, Santa Maria, (Named after Mary, mother of Jesus), was discovered by Goncalo Velho Cabral. Cabral had been trained at the school founded by Prince Henry the Navigator (1394-1460), and had been commissioned to *"discover some land and return with notice."* [20] He did so over the next ten years, discovering island after island of the Azores archipelago. According to most scholars, Terceira was

---

[20] Gavet-Imbert, M., (Ed), (1999). *The Guinness Book of Explorers and Exploration.* Enfield, Middlesex Great Britain: Guinness Publishing, LTD.

discovered by Goncalo Velho Cabral in 1437 with the naming of the island, "Formigas," alternatively, others attribute the discovery to Cabral's pilot, Vicente de Lagos in 1445, when he named the island, *"The Island of Jesus Christ,"* because he discovered the island on the 1st of January, the feast day of the name of Jesus. He also was of the Military Order of Christ similar to the Knights Templars of the past and he desired that legacy to continue. Many of these early explorers were highly religious, and since Lagos and Cabral were both men of faith, with Cabral being both a monk and an explorer, many factors contributed to this push by these explorers and the Portuguese Crown to find and conquer new lands. In the Bible, in the Gospel of Matthew 28:16, Jesus had told his disciples, *"Therefore go and make disciples of all nations, baptizing them in the name of the Father and the Son and of the Holy Spirit, and teaching them to obey everything I have commanded you....."* (NIV).[21] In taking this command literally, both Lagos and Cabral, in the name of Christ and in the name of the Crown, conquered. This resulted in them being confused and conflicted at times as to the nature of their exploration which mixed religion, politics, and commerce, similar to what future explorers did as well. Despite this, Cabral was given later given the title, "Commander of the Islands of the Azores," due to his virtues and trustworthiness. He was trained at the school founded by Henry the Navigator, the most famous of all Portuguese explorers.

---

[21] *Holy Bible, New International Version.* (1983). Grand Rapids, Michigan: Zondervan Bible Publishers.

Prince Henry the Navigator

Prince Henry the Navigator, who was the fourth son of King John I of Portugal, had trained many men at the nautical school that he founded in Sagres, Portugal, where he enlisted cartographers, historians, ship captains, geographers, and even monks to begin this "Age of Exploration." Prince Henry was a highly religious and pious man, never marrying and never fathering any children, thereby staying continually focused on his exploration and his search for new knowledge. He was also the Grand Master of the Military Order of Christ. Prince Henry looked to the Atlantic for his exploits, especially to the South Atlantic along the coast of Africa, to fulfill this Biblical commission and also to fill the coffers of the crown with the riches drawn from Africa. The island of Terceira, while not being on the route south to Africa, was nevertheless along the oceanic gulf stream that flowed north to their home in Portugal. This greatly contributed to Terceira's discovery. (The gulf stream is also the reason the weather in Terceira stays temperate all year long).

When Terceira island was first named and documented it was

called, Formigas, and then later, The Island of Christ, but soon thereafter was changed to Terceira, or Third Island, in reference to the fact that it was the third island of the Azores to be found by the Portuguese. Whoever was the first authentic discoverer has remained a mystery to this day, but we do know it was a Portuguese navigator, nonetheless. We are not certain if Henry the Navigator himself came to Terceira, but we know for sure that it was under his tutelage that the discovery was made. [22]

Age of Colonization

As was customary in the colonization of islands by the Portuguese, livestock of goats, pigs, donkeys, and cows would immediately be introduced to ensure a supply of meat, milk, and transport upon return. The administration would be handed over to a governor or "Capitao Donatario," a captain in military terms. He would administer the defense, the allocation of land use, land ownership, and the judicial system to be implemented.

In 1450, Prince Henry gave the administration of the island into the hands of a Flemish nobleman by the name of Jacome de Bruges to govern on his behalf. Bruges, along with seventeen families, resettled to Terceira in what is known today as Porto Juneau. Today the Flemish occupy about half of the population of Belgium and still have their own ethnic identity in Belgium, The Netherlands, and France, but those that came to colonize Terceira mainly came from the Flanders area of Northern Europe and have integrated fully into the life of Terceira. The Flemish brought livestock, and seeds for planting, and soon began commercial enterprises that encouraged development. They embarked with their livestock and provisions in the area of Porto Juneau and began to settle along the southern coast. The settlers spread throughout the island establishing business

---

[22] Wolf, E., (1982). *Europe and the People Without History*. Los Angeles: University of California Press.

ventures in the areas of agriculture, forestry, wool production, sugar distilleries, and later introducing tobacco, tea, and citrus for export.

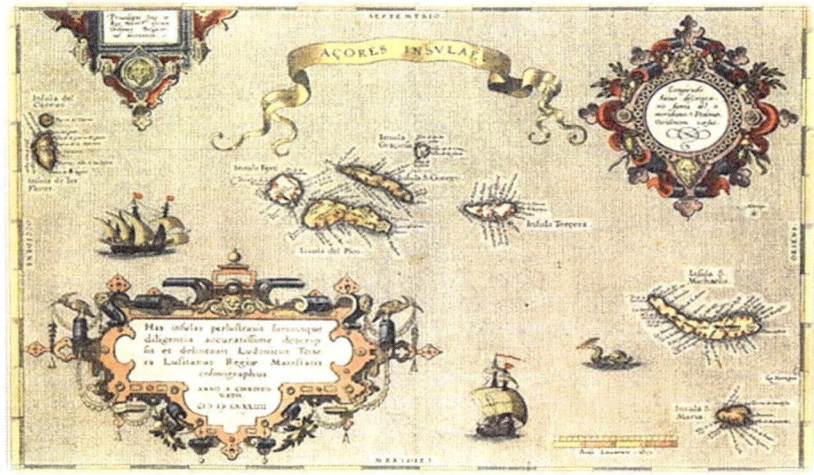

1584 Map of the Azores

Bruges continued to bring in new Flemish settlers along with colonists from Madeira Island, slaves from Africa, Portuguese immigrants, and even Jews. (Jews were still a viable community on Terceira until 1998 when the last of the Jewish population immigrated to Israel.) Later, Bruges would move to Praia da Vitoria and establish the administrative center of the island there because of the port facilities and easy access. By the end of the 14th century, the island would be home to over two thousand Flemish settlers. Their influence can still be seen today by the presence of their windmills, the making of lace, and their cuisine. Ethnically you will also see the Flemish influence on the island as portrayed in the blue-eyed and blond-haired children of Terceira.

Since the Flemish were Roman Catholics, as were the Portuguese, they worshipped together and early on built Catholic churches and religious monuments in their settlements. The Matriz Church or the Church of Sao Sebastiao built in 1456 is the oldest church in Terceira. It was built by Jacome de Bruges and can still be visited today.

The Matriz Church

Jacob de Bruges

Many years later, the capital of the island would move to Angra do Heroismo, where it remains to this day. In 1474, Bruges upon a return trip to Flanders disappeared never to be heard of again, and his disappearance remains a mystery. Some say he was murdered; others say that he was lost at sea, and others say he died of old age in an undisclosed location as he tried to escape from his scorned lovers. (After all, he did father two illegitimate sons, and two legitimate daughters, and was married numerous times). After his death, the island was divided into two captaincies or governmental centers, with one being at Angra, under the auspices of Joao Vaz Corte Real, and the other being, Praia, under the supervision of Alvaro Martins Homem. [23]

In the 15th and 16th centuries, Terceira, as a port-of-call, became a trading post for the Americas with the Portuguese colonies bringing in spices, gold, silver, timber, precious jewels, and African slaves. As the largest permanent settlement on the island, Angra was a city of significant importance because of its harbor and the Spanish fortresses that protected it. It was to grow into a city of great wealth and commerce. Today, it has still retained its importance, for in 1983 it was declared a UNESCO site due to its role in the development of the new world.

By the late 1400s, Terceira, as a colony of Portugal, began to reap the harvest of Portuguese trade. In 1444 the first human cargo, black slaves from the African coast, had been brought to Lisbon along with gold and ivory. They would later be shipped to the Americas by way of the Azores. The islands of the Canaries, Cape Verde, and the Azores were all being colonized and with the importation of sugar cane, olives, and grapevines, they, along with mainland Portugal, were moving from being the poor man of the Iberian peninsula to the rich man of Europe. All of Europe was

---

[23] *Jacome de Bruges*. Retrieved 1/21/21 from http://en.wikipedia.org/wiki/Jacome_de_Bruges.

taking notice and each wanted a piece of the riches being traded.

Columbus Discovers America

This was not the end of this century of exploration, for, in 1492, another sea captain of Portuguese descent by the name of Christopher Columbus would make his mark on the history of the Azores and the Island of Terceira. Columbus upon his return to Spain on February 15, 1493, carried with him the news that he had "discovered" America. However, after being driven off course by violent storms, he landed not in the Canaries as proposed, but at Santa Maria, the first island in the Azores archipelago.[24] They put in at the harbor of the village of Anjos, "Our Lady of the Angels," and Columbus sent in ten men from the Nina's one small boat to proclaim their intent. Columbus expected that the men would immediately return with good news, but after some time, no sailor was to be seen. They thought they would be welcomed, but the governor of the island, not knowing from where they had sailed, jailed Columbus and his crew, assuming they were pirates and smugglers. Upon further documentation, it was found that he indeed had been commissioned and credentialed to sail under the King of Spain, and he and his crew were released. They were given provisions and an offer of hospitality. Upon their release in an act of

---

[24] Litivinoff, B., (1991). 1492 *The Decline of Medievalism and the Rise of the Modern Age*. New York: Macmillan Publishing Co.

penitence and thanksgiving, they held their religious devotions in the nearest chapel which can still be seen today on Santa Maria island. After leaving Santa Maria, Columbus still had eight hundred miles left to go before reaching the mainland, but on March 4th he entered the harbor of Lisbon, and at forty-one years of age, he was considered the supreme explorer of the century having done what no other had done before. [25]

Later, Columbus would continue his travels and it is reported by the Inca historian, Garcilasso de la Vega, that Columbus lived for a while on the island of Terceira. In 1609, Garcilasso wrote that a ship pilot by the name of Alonzo Sanchez of Huelva, as he sailed from the Canaries to Madeira in 1484, was caught in a violent storm and driven off course and landed in Santa Domingo. Upon his return to the European mainland from Santa Domingo, he landed on Terceira, where he along with five others, were received by Columbus in his own house in Angra. Some say this is only conjecture, but others claim that the document is real, and the facts are true. As of yet, this particular house that was the residence of Columbus has not been identified. [26] Today, there is a house identified as Columbus' house in Genoa, Italy, as well as a house on the island of Porto Santo. Porto Santo is one of the islands of the Madeiras and the house there currently houses the Columbus museum, but as of yet, no house has firmly been identified as the house of Columbus in the city of Angra do Heriosmo.

On May 2oth, 1506, Columbus died in Valladolid, Spain, but later his remains would be moved to a monastery on La Cartuga, an island next to Seville. Columbus was a deeply religious man and he conquered under the name of the crown and the name of Christ, his

---

[25] Foster, G., (1965). *The World of Columbus and Sons*. San Luis Obispo, California: Beautiful Feet Books.
[26] Thacher, J., (2021). *Christopher Columbus: His Life, His Works, His Remains*. Great Britain: Alpha Editions Publishing Company.

Lord. In his will, he wrote, *"I presented (to Spain) the Indies. I say presented, because it is evident that by the will of God, our Sovereign, I gave them, as a thing that was mine."* [27] Columbus was reported to be a converted Jew or what was called a "conversos" and thusly, as a devout Christian, wanted to win the world for Christ. [28]

Today, some of Columbus' physical remains also lie in the Dominican Republic in the Columbus Lighthouse mausoleum inaugurated in 1992 in tribute to Columbus. It is a large memorial building in the form of a cross that was constructed in time for the 500th year anniversary of the discovery of the Americas.

1492 was not only important for Columbus and the Americas but for Terceira as well. In 1492, the first hospital of the Azores was built on March 15th of that year in Angra. It was built with the support of Confraria do Santo Espirito (Brotherhood of the Holy Spirit), and one of the founders of the Brotherhood was Captain of Angra and the discoverer of Newfoundland, Joao Vaz Corte-Real. The Misericordia Church of Angra is situated today on the earlier location of the hospital which moved in the 19th century.

It is strange, but in storytelling, islands always conjure up a mystery and a fascination, and for years if some animal or creature is thought to be extinct, or some race of people that is lost, they always seem to exist on a deserted island. With the discovery of Terceira, that mystery or intrigue is now mostly forgotten. However, it is possible that the mystery of Columbus' house in Angra, along with the folk tales of old, the legend of Atlantis, and the pre-history of Terceira will create tantalizing tales of the high seas alive for years to come.

Taking a walk down historic memory lane in Terceira is like

---

[27] Lyon, E., (1992, January). Search for Columbus. *National Geographic*.
[28] Armstrong, K. (2000). The Battle for God. New York, New York: Alfred A. Knoff Publishing.

walking through textbooks of old and finding buried treasures. Characters jump out and catch you with the realism that exists not only in ancient texts but also in their lives and the meaning that surrounds us. It is a feeling that a tourist senses as one walks the streets of Angra, Praia, and the villages that line the seashore.

Vasco da Gama

Other notable people would also visit Terceira before the end of the 14th century such as the famous Portuguese explorer, Vasco da Gama, who visited Terceira in 1499. He came to visit his brother, and while visiting Terceira, his brother, Paulo, turned ill and died. He died in Angra and is buried in the monastery of Sao Francisco. Upon his brother's death, Vasco da Gama left Terceira and returned to Portugal in September of the year 1499.[29] Vasco da Gama is most famously known for his initial sailing trip to India that linked the Atlantic and the Pacific Oceans by way of the Cape of Good Hope, South Africa.

Later in 1534, Angra was officially declared to be a city and it became the headquarters of the government, commerce, religious

---

[29] Editors of Encyclopedia Britannica. *Terceira Island*, Retrieved 1/7/22 from http://www.britannica.com/science/island.

activity, and the main stop for intercontinental travel. It was filled with spices, gold, jewels, wood, and slaves. The nations of Britain, France, and Spain began to take notice, and because of the fear of sabotage and piracy, the Portuguese trading ships would gather in Angra and then move in a mass convoy to Portugal, protected by warships as they made their way to Lisbon. All of that would change when Spanish annexed Portugal in 1580 and the Spanish King, Filipe II, took over the throne of Portugal and declared the Azores to be a Spanish protectorate. However, the people of Terceira declared their allegiance to D. Antonio, Prior of Crato, as their rightful King and held out in rebellion. Over the next two years, with the Battle of Salga in 1581 and then with additional violent clashes with the Spanish, the Island of Terceira was finally taken, and the last stronghold of the Azores was defeated by the armies of Spain. The people of Terceira have always maintained an independent spirit and throughout their history, in contrast with the other islands of the Azores, have sought freedom and independence from all outside forces.

From 1640 to 1668, the Portuguese waged the "Portuguese Restoration War" and finally in 1668, Spain recognized the independence of Portugal, and Terceira was once again under Portuguese domination. Portuguese kings and monarchies would rise and fall in Portugal, catching Terceira in a complex net of intrigues, counterinsurgencies, and political ideologies. King Alfonso would declare himself King in 1656, only to be disposed of by his brother, King Peter (Dom Pedro II) in 1683 with Alfons being exiled to Terceira for the next seven years. There was the typical behind the throne scrambling for power with both the mother of Alfons, Louisa Maria, and her consorts, vying for power in opposition to the kings' wives as the ladies in waiting.

In Portugal, this back and forth fighting between Spain, Britain, France, and Portugal would continue with the result that the Azores, and Terceira in particular, would constantly be in an upheaval. Some administrative reforms would occur during this time and the Azores would be declared a province of Portugal with Angra as its capital, thus catapulting Terceira to the forefront of political aspirations again. During the 1800s, Terceira would be ruled by various factions such as the English Marshall, William Beresford, and a Portuguese King whose capital was actually in Brazil. It was all very confusing as Europe went from monarchies to democracies. It still is a little confusing today as well.

Likewise in the 1800s, Terceira would again be challenged as Portugal broke into two political factions, the "Liberals" and the "Abolitionists." This would cause division not just between the Azores and Portugal, but between individual islands of the archipelago. Each island was seeking various degrees of autonomy and Terceira was caught in conflict again having sided with the "Liberals." Back and forth the political climate went, changing views and kings, regents, and governments, almost as often as the weather of Terceira changes. There were protests, persecutions, upheavals, uprisings, betrayals, and constant infighting. Terceira would continue to play an important role in Portuguese politics with the Duke of Terceira taking control of all of Portugal in 1834. It would be over a hundred years later before Portugal would again be confronted with a major political decision.

For many years since the early colonization of Terceira, the island had been a gem in the Atlantic for the weary sailor looking for a rest and a port of call. However, as aviation developed, the Azores again would be utilized for that initial air crossing of the Atlantic. In May 1919, the first transatlantic flight took place with a critical stopover at the island of Faial. Later in 1928, the first airport on Terceira would be built using only packed earth as the runway. It would be abandoned soon thereafter due to its size and adverse weather conditions. Again, in 1934 another site was chosen, and the airport now known as Lajes Field would be completed. It would prove to be a vital staging area for troops and military hardware for the Allied effort during WWII.

During WWII, Portugal would decide to remain neutral at the beginning of the war, but later they would join the Allies, allowing the English navy the use of its ports and the Americans the use of its airfields. Early on, the airfield on the Island of Santa Maria would be used as a stopping place for bombers to land and refuel before finishing the remainder of the trip to England, but towards the end of the war, Lajes would rise to the occasion and become the primary airport for the Allies to occupy and conduct both air and sea operations. From there supplies and military cargo, as well as British and American aircraft, would operate. The island of Terceira would prove to be of significant importance to the war effort as 8,689 U.S. aircraft would pass through Lajes on their way to assist in the defeating of the Nazis. *("A Short History of Lajes Field"* is an excellent book on the military history of Lajes) Along with the American aircraft, British airmen would also use the field, with each adding their names to the heroes who flew from there. (My father, Robert Tilley, would be one of the B-17 pilots who used Lajes as a stopover before arriving in England. Later, I, the author would also pass through Lajes, then my sons, Robert and Jason: three generations of honorary Terceira islanders.)

Lajes airfield would also play a vital role in the transport of returning troops from the battlefield back to the U.S.A. Many a young soldier would remember the island of Terceira as a place of safety far from the wounds of war. Terceira became home to soldiers, sailors, and airmen alike.

But the airfield's role would not end there, for it also participated in the Berlin Airlift of 1948, the Arab-Israeli Conflict of 1973, the Gulf War, and numerous humanitarian operations that assisted many in the North Atlantic. Today, only a remnant of airmen remain at Lajes Airfield as its mission has changed due to technological advances and new political coalitions, but the history of the base will remain in servicemen's memories for many years to come.[30]

Terceira was again in the timeline of international history with the historical district of Angra do Heroismo being declared a UNESCO World Heritage Site in 1983. Then in 1986, Portugal joined the European Union, which would propel Terceira economically into a fully functional addition to Europe. Tourism would explode and exports rise as Terceira would send its agricultural and dairy products to the far reaches of Europe.

Today, Terceira's history continues to be written as it becomes a major destination for tourists and businesses alike with its multitude of environmentally friendly attractions and its rich historical background.

---

[30] A Short History of Lajes Field, Terceira Island, Azores, Portugal.

Chapter Three
Tourism in Terceira:

Major Tourist Attractions

Terceira has been at the forefront of the 21st century by promoting and assisting in implementing environmentally sustainable green tourism. The government of Terceira has long understood that if Terceira is going to maintain its place as a prime tourist destination, then its tourism must be controlled by more than just economic factors. Tourism must be tied to the natural beauty of Terceira and managed both from a business and a green model of development. Up to now, they have done just that. When you come to Terceira you feel that you are not a tourist, but part of the larger Terceira family. The people are friendly, the beaches are not overcrowded, and the prices of food and lodging are moderately priced. Healthcare is present and easily accessible, and transportation, whether by bus or rental car, is functional and easy to access. It is an ideal place to relax, enjoy nature, and immerse yourself in the joys of this beautiful island.

As it would be impossible to list all of the attractions available, this book will highlight the most popular attractions and tourist destinations. Experiences such as whale watching, scuba diving, photo tours, and guided nature hikes will be found at most tourist outlets. There are sandy beaches, volcanic rock swimming inlets, mountain trails, craggy streams, and forested picnic areas to be enjoyed without cost or crowds. Historic museums abound and gastronomic delights are found around every corner. You will also be surprised to find "fast food" chains if that is your desire, but from experience, local food in your neighborhood cafes cannot be beaten.

Terceira has something for everyone. Whether you are an adventurer hiking through extinct volcanic craters, or a child playing in the sand on the beach, Terceira is the place for you. If you simply want to relax at a corner coffee shop and drink expressos, then there is a good shop right in the heart of Angra that is classic and inexpensive at the same time. It is a place where you can people watch if you are inclined, or you can spend the day, drinking your coffee and reading your favorite novel. There is an ambiance of safety, peace, and security, all for your enjoyment.

So, come and let the adventure begin:

Let us first let us go over a few rules that will make your trip to Terceira more pleasant, especially in areas of natural beauty. It is forbidden:

1. *To introduce, catch, capture, handle, or to hold any animal*

or plant species that are endangered.
2. To exploit any geological resource.
3. To drop litter.
4. To cut trees or to change vegetation in any way.
5. To practice sports that may damage the environment.
6. To engage in any activity that could disturb the ecological equilibrium of any protected area.
7. To smoke inside of natural designated natural zones.[31]

Before we look at the designated areas of interest and the attractions themselves, let us examine some of the various activities that one can do while on Terceira. Most of the activities and tours are organized by licensed tourist agencies, but many of the activities you can enjoy singularly on your own cognizance. Just make sure you get permission before you cross private land that is not designated as a touristic zone. Locals are very friendly, but they are quite concerned if you leave gates open, fences down, and interact with the livestock in an abusive fashion. Always leave the landscape in a better condition than when you found it.

Categories of Tours and Services

You will find an assortment of tours, services, classes, and assistance in the following sports and activities.

- *Canyoning* – Canyoning with the help of a guide with adequate ropes and equipment will enable the young and old to climb and rappel down numerous waterfalls, volcanic crevices, and craggy outcrops. Most noted for adventurers is the area of rivers and trails in the Ribeira da Agualva.

---

[31] Terceira Island Environmental Department

- *Hiking* – Whether a person likes to hike through the Enchanted Forrest of Serreta or along the rim of an extinct volcano, hiking trails abound. Some are graded as to their difficulty and length, so it is best to know your endurance level before proceeding. Also, be aware that the weather on Terceira can change each hour so adequate rain gear is a necessity.

- *Swimming* – Ocean swimming can be taken either at the

beach in Praia de Victoria, or at the small beach at the port in Angra do Heroismo. However, caution must be taken to avoid the changing tides and ocean currents that constantly change as per the weather. Whether in winter or summer, you can always take advantage of the beaches for sunbathing and picnics with the family. There are also tidal pools located in most of the villages along the seafront which utilize the natural formation of bays and inlets for swimming as the sea crashes over your head forming waves that envelope your body. Most popular is the village of Biscoites (Biscuits) where the natural pools are easily accessible and have adequate

parking and functional facilities that are present.

- *Scuba Diving* – Dive shops are dotted across the island where licensed scuba divers can rent equipment for a minimal fee. Scuba diving courses by certified PADI instructors are also available for the novice diver. The clear waters around Terceira are filled with all sorts of colorful marine life, from eagle rays and stingrays to a multitude of iridescent fish not unlike those found in the tropics. Larger marine animals such as porpoises and whales also make their home in the waters around Terceira as well. If you are more adventurous then diving in old shipwrecks, or diving for new archaeological discoveries may be just what is needed to add spice to your profile. The finding of sunken treasures may just check off another point on your "bucket list."

- *Whale Watching* – Whaling in the Azores has been outlawed for many years which in turn has caused the abundance of whales to increase throughout the Azores. There are over twenty-seven species of whales and dolphins (porpoises) that inhabit the surrounding waters. Many sightings of these large marine animals can be seen from the shore, but to get the maximum effect, a trip by boat out among the biggest mammals on earth is awe-inspiring.

- *Fishing* – Fishing aboard a chartered fishing boat will always bring in a daily catch of fresh fish for the palette. You do not have to be a professional to pull in some trophies, as locals know all the right spots to take advantage of this sport. You can always fish from the shore and with the assistance of the local villagers, who know when the catch is in, will teach you how to bake or fry the fish that was caught personally by you.

- *Archaeological Tours and Discovery* – Today, much is still being learned about the early history of Terceira and with a local guide you too can explore the early remains of tombs, artifacts, monuments, and caves dating back to prehistoric times. Since much of the prehistorical sites are still under evaluation, care must be taken so as to not disturb the ruins and artifacts that continue to be found.

- *Photography* – Around every corner of Terceira there are

vistas and panoramic views that will entice the most avid photographer. Sunset and rainbows can be seen daily, which along with the interaction of land and sea, will provide photo opportunities that film alone cannot capture. The vast array of greens and their contrasting colors, together with the light shimmering off the azure ocean waves will keep your attention captivated for hours. It is a photographic paradise.

- *Geological Adventures* – Since Terceira abounds with geological formations that will bring out your childhood fantasies of volcanoes, dinosaurs (not present today for sure), caves, and unexplored calderas, an exploration of more than an afternoon is needed. There are crater lakes, fumarolic fields, algares, volcanic vents, and lava fields which are sure to bring out the child in you once again. The most popular touristic destination of this nature is the Algar do Carvao Regional Natural Monument which is visited by both cavers and hikers alike.

- *Land and Boat Tours* – In addition to all the experiences listed above, jeep tours, ATV adventures, a boat by night or glass-bottom boat explorations, and all-day bus tours are available.

- *Horseback Riding* – There are stables and horse-riding trails that dot the island. Tourists can rent horses and also get instructions as to how to ride. Off-road trails abound that are open to horse riders as well as catered tours that accompany the rider with gastronomical cuisine and cheeses made locally just for the occasion.

- *Golfing* – The golf course at Terceira will certainly rival any course you may have played on. The forest and greens merge together into one symphony of peace and tranquility that will make your golfing experience a joy to remember. There is the Terceira Island Golf Club that caters to all your golfing needs as well as the golf club restaurant with panoramic vistas and catered food.

Main Tourist Sites

Algar do Carvao and the Furnas do Enxofre Hiking Trail

Probably the most visited tourist site in Terceira is the Grota Algar do Carvao. It is a volcanic vent or tube where one can climb into the throat of an inactive volcanic pit. The vent is 17m x 27m in size and the corresponding conduit drops 45m from the surface. It then drops vertically again into a lake that is filled with crystal clear rainwater. The walls and roof are covered with a beautiful, stunning, multi-colored obsidian, almost glassy in appearance, which draws your eyes upward as you gaze at the sunlight pouring in. You enter the monument through a narrow tunnel to arrive at this magnificent theater formed thousands of years ago. As water is filtered through the subsoil, stalactites, and stalagmites of silica form, adding another dimension to the already gorgeous interior. Upon descending to the bottom of the cave through a series of stepped walkways you will be greeted by a lake 15m in depth that only adds to the tropical feel of the entire complex. There is water dripping as tiny droplets from the roof, which along with the smell of the peat mosses growing inside the conduit, gives the feeling that you are in a rain forest in the Amazon basin. It is no wonder that this is a popular tourist destination on Terceira. It is located in the center of the island, 550m above sea level in the Regional Natural Monument.

The cave complex is also home to a variety of unique plant and animal life. In the deeper parts of the cave, there exist species of algae, diatoms, and mold that have adapted to underground life. In the conduit itself, there are over thirty-four species of mushrooms, twenty-two species of moss, and twenty-seven vascular plants including ferns. Some of these plants exist only on the Azores and can be found in just a few spots not touched by human hands. Some insects have made this cave their home such as the beetle (Trechus terceiranus) endemic only to Terceira, as well as two spider species. Some birds can be seen in the mouth of the cave that are native only to the Azores as well, specifically, the Azores chaffinch.

*There are a few things that happily do not exist on Terceira. There are no snakes on the island and no animals, exotic or not, that are harmful to human life. That is not to say that the sea surrounding the island is safe, for there are species of jellyfish that you do not want to touch. They can inflict pain, paralysis, and even death, so be informed before you touch them.

It is advisable to check the times that the Grota is open before you visit as times are subject to change.

Adjacent to the cave complex, a circular trail leading to Furnas do Enxofre starts in the parking lot at Algar. The trail-rated medium is 6.2km in length and takes approximately two and a half hours to complete. It leads to a fumarole field where hot gases of hydrogen sulfide and carbon dioxide are being emitted through still active volcanic fissures. Much of the trail is on elevated walkways, so there is no danger from the gases, but it is advised to strictly stay on the trail for your safety. The trail takes you through the Pico Alto volcanic field with amazing views and in an environmentally protected area of a nature preserve.[32]

Conduit at Algar do Carvao

Biscoitos and the Malba Grande Hiking Trail

Located on the north side of the island is a small village known for its natural pools where locals and tourists alike go to swim in the ocean. There are a variety of pools, both in-depth and in ease of access, which caters to the novice swimmer. For those that are more

---

[32] *Algar do Carvao, Terceira, Azores*. Retrieved 2/16/22 from http: sram.azores.gov.pt.

proficient in the sport, open pools are available that will challenge your skills as you combat the surf and waves. There is plenty of parking at the swimming "hole" as well as refreshments, an outdoor café, and a restaurant. There are additional eating establishments serving local cuisine throughout the village of Biscoitos.

Biscoitos is also home to the Wine Museum of Terceira, where they highlight the local vineyards, the wines, and the process of distilling the wine. The museum is open every day except Mondays, but check the schedule as it may change seasonally. They have a variety of displays that highlight the history of winemaking on Terceira and the various tools used, the distillery, and the wine cellar. They have a wine tasting room and a gift shop.

Biscoitos is also home to many "bed and breakfast" rentals that are built with native stone and are of traditional style and structure. Prices are reasonably priced, but reservations are needed.

The area also boasts of a beautiful hiking trail, the Malba Grande trail, which is a circular route of 14.2km and is rated medium. It is a trail with varied impressions of pastoral fields complete with the iconic black and white dairy cows of Terceira, old orchards, wooded hills, and verdant valleys of streams and ferns. Along the trail, you will also see the trenches left from WWII built in defense of the island. The trail connects to the Rocha da Chambre viewpoint that gives you panoramic vistas all the way to the sea and beyond to the next corresponding island.

Tidal Swim Pool at Biscoitos

Serreta Hiking Trail and the Mata da Serreta Park

There are many hiking trails throughout the island, but the Serreta trail at the northwest corner of the island is awe-inspiring and is a place of particular natural beauty. It is a looped trail of 6.7km (4.2 miles) with the trailhead beginning close to the village of Serreta. The trail is rated as moderate in its descent and difficulty and is well marked. The trail takes you through a large grove of Japanese Red Cedar, past a small lagoon, and a lake that sits in the crater of an inactive volcano. It leads you up to beautiful vistas overlooking both land and sea. The trail crisscrosses a forest reserve leading you through eucalyptus, cedar, pine, and laurel trees as well as other foliage that is endemic to Terceira.

Close to the trail is another tourist site; Mata da Serreta. Although the site is not classified as a trail, but more of a walk, it leads you into a park surrounded by luxuriant trees that abound with an aroma that will envelop your senses. It is one of the first nature parks built on Terceira and is complete with a children's play area, bathrooms, and a shelter for picnics. It has a beautiful fountain that once stood in the Graca Covent, in Angra do Heroismo. The park is open all year at no cost, and if the weather is right you can see across the ocean to the other islands of Graciosa and Sao Jorge.

The village of Serreta is also known for the Festa of Nossa Senhora dos Milagres, a pilgrimage that is attended by local islanders each year to commemorate, "Our Lady of the Miracles." People from all over the island gather for this festival with food and drink, and with prayers and supplications to come to the Chapel at Serreta. The chapel is named after an event that happened in the 17th century when a priest was saved from danger by a painting of the "Lady of Miracles." As a token of appreciation, the priest built a small chapel for which to house the painting in what is today, Serreta. After the death of the priest, the painting was removed and placed in a church in the village of Doze Ribeiras. However, in 1842, the painting was once again brought back to Serreta and since then the festival is held yearly. The present chapel that you see today in Serreta dates back to 1902.

The cult of the "Lady of Miracles" is as much folklore as religion, but it is a highly revered pilgrimage to this day. People from all over the island will make the walk with some walking as many as 80km to come to Serreta to make a petition for protection, health, or wealth. Some just come to offer thanks to God for the blessings that they experienced in the past year. The Serreta pilgrimage is both a religious feast and a time for social bonding for the people of Terceira where young and old, rich and poor can come together for one weekend and feel the peace of God and the friendship of neighbors. It is a time when communion with God is sought, and the community of man is experienced too. If you happen to be in Terceira in September make sure you go and enjoy this pilgrimage as well, as you too seek to find wholeness both in body and soul.

As a whole, Terceira is predominately Roman Catholic, and as such, every village has a church, many dating back hundreds of years. Catholicism was one of the motivating factors leading to the exploration by the Portuguese as they sought to Christianize the unknown world. Sometimes, much criticism has been directed against the Catholic Church because of this, but to be intellectually honest, where the church went, hospitals went, schools went, music went, and of course, churches went. The church on Terceira is a uniting point tying festivals, holidays, and families together. One of the first things you will notice on your first trip to Terceira is the lack of crime, the lack of hostility, and the feeling of calmness and peace you get from the local population. It is all tied to religious upbringing and the teachings of Christ when he said, *"You shall love the Lord your God with all your heart, with all your soul, and with all your strength, and with all your mind, and your neighbor as yourself."* (Luke 10:27). [33] Your enjoyment of this island is because the locals are enjoying you, their families, and their God.

Fountain at the Park of Mata da Serreta

---

[33] *Holy Bible, New International Version.* (1983). Grand Rapids, Michigan: Zondervan Bible Publishers.

Misterios Negros Hiking Trail and Gruta do Natal (Christmas Cave)

The trail at Misterios Negros (Dark Mysteries) is 4.9km and takes around two hours and thirty minutes to hike. It begins near the Lagoa do Negros (Dark Lake) and the Gruta do Natal (Christmas Cave) which are located in the middle of the island. On this trail, you can explore the dark lava rock formations and various lagoons, including the Lagoa dos Misterios Negros and the three lakes of Lagoinhas do Val Fundo. You will also pass the black volcanic trachytic domes left from the eruption of 1761 and experience a variety of foliage endemic to Terceira. The trail is rated difficult in its hiking level as its circular route encompasses lofty peaks, craggy valleys, and steep inclines.

The trail is located within the Special Preservation Area or Natural Reserve of Santa Barbara. It ends at the Gruta do Natal, which is one of the three tourist caves on Terceira. The main attraction there is the 700m lava tube that was left after a volcanic eruption. The tube is easy to walk inside, and other geological formations such as lava flows and small lateral fissures can also be seen. It is a great place to better understand the formation of Terceira and its volcanic origins. The trail ends at the Gruta do Natal, which is one of the three tourist caves on Terceira. You can view Gruta do Natal without any hiking involved if you so desire, and there is ample parking for your attention. There is also a picnic area at Lagoa do Negro which is free of charge. If you are planning to hike this trail as well as visit the Christmas Cave, then an entire afternoon will be needed. Again, always have rain gear as you never know when the weather may change.

Baias de Agualva Hiking Trail

The trail at Agualva is the shortest of all guided trails on Terceira being only 3.8km in length. It is a linear route and rated as a moderate trail in difficulty and takes two hours to complete. The trail is along the north coast and there are many panoramic vistas comprising both sea and volcanic landscapes. In the village of Agualva itself, you will find adequate refreshments to assist you on your walk. There is also a picnic area in the village. The bays along the trail with the waves splashing and the sun shining will provide many mini rainbows in the ocean surf that will engage your imagination and take you back to your childhood dreams of adventure. Just be careful on the rocky ledges as they may be slippery and wet, and an accidental mishap could occur. Be sure to wear footgear that matches the type of trail that your adventure takes. All trails are marked by red and yellow markers that will take you to your destination.

Passegem das Bestes Hiking Trail

This trail is one of the most interesting trails on Terceira as it passes over the "Passage of the Beasts" ox-cart ruts which have been contested for many years as to their origin and their age. Interestingly, even Charles Darwin, during his stop in Terceira when he was traveling aboard the "Beagle" sailing vessel, made mention of these ancient ox-cart ruts. He compared them to Roman roads that appear to be similar in construction. However, today, you can hike to the very spot where these ruts are seen as they trek across the Terceira landscape. The trail is 4km in length and the entire trail can be hiked in about three hours. It is a circular trail and is of medium difficulty. Not only will you be able to examine the ox-cart ruts, but you will also pass-through groves of Japanese Cedars, Azorean heather, and Azorean cedars. You will be able to view one of the most impressive vistas in all of the Azores as you experience the view of the Cino Picos caldera that is situated between Sierra da Rebeirinha and Serra do Cume. It is the largest caldera in all of the Azore Islands as it is over 7km in diameter.

Rocha do Chambre Hiking Trail

The Rocha do Chambre trail is 8.8 km long and takes about three hours to traverse. It is rated as a medium trail in difficulty. The main attraction on this trail is the vertical cliff called the "Giant Chambre's Rock." It is a massive cliff where the volcano collapsed along a fault line leaving behind a massive rock outcropping that rises off of the crater floor. As on other trails throughout Terceira, the trail crosses through groves of cedars and lush green pastures, over streams and crevices, to give you an invigorating hike that can be enjoyed in one afternoon. There are gates through which you must pass, and the local farmers only ask that you close and lock the gates leaving them as you found them. Also, it is noted that in some pastures there may be bulls that if approached, may get aggressive and leave an impression that would not be so favorable. "Leave the bulls alone" would be the best advice, and do not endeavor to be the bullfighting tourist that ends up taking a souvenir home that stays with you forever. Leave the bullfighting to those that know it best and be careful that you do not entice the bulls to an encounter.

Relheiras de Sao Bras Hiking Trail

Starting at the picnic area in the village in Sao Bras and proceeding to the monument that honors ancient oxcarts, the trail begins and travels in a circular pattern for the next 5km. It is a trail easily accessible as about half of the trail follows a wide road and the other half takes you through an almost mystical forest. You feel like you have stepped back in time as the trail crosses the ox-cart tracks laid down hundreds, maybe even thousands, of years ago as seen in the vertical V-shaped ruts, and the broader, flat-shaped ruts that were left behind. Some say they are similar to the famous ruts seen in Malta, therefore making them megalithic in time, while others have said they are like ruts that the Romans left in Switzerland and Spain. Much discussion as to their origin is still being argued in the academic community. (see the picture of ruts on page 9).

Lagoa da Patas and the Grande Rota do Oeste Hiking Trail

Along the highway that runs through the middle of the island is a fairyland park that caters to both young and old alike. There is a playground for the children, a shelter for group outings, picnic tables, an artificial lake, a pond filled with ducks waiting for a treat, and a free-flowing stream that runs out of the Forest Reserve of Santa Barbara. It is known locally as the "duck pond," but it is more than that. It is a lake surrounded by azaleas, hydrangeas, ferns, Japanese cedars, and other foliage endemic to Terceira. It is a cool misty place in the summer where the children can run free, and the adults relax. The ducks, which appear to be always hungry, continue to entertain with their antics and color. In the spring, the baby ducks in their yellow down keep you mesmerized for hours. It is both a tourist destination and a local hangout for families and friends. It is also the beginning of the trailhead of the hiking trail, "Grande Rota do Oeste." It is a trail of 31.2km that runs along the western edge of

Terceira. It passes through valleys and hills, villages, and markets. Because of its length, it is better to take the trail in two parts as it is probably too strenuous for those that are not professional hikers. There are places to stop and rest, have a picnic, and even bed and breakfast accommodations to stop and spend the night. The hike in its entirety will take approximately ten hours to complete, but it is advisable to not try and complete it at one time. It is a linear hike and is rated as difficult because of its length and the elevated nature of some of the inclines. Take along plenty of water, and it is advisable to have a hiking partner just in case of an emergency.

Lagoa das Patas

Fortes de Sao Sebastiao Hiking Trail

This trail, unlike most other trails that take you through the interior of the island, is filled with history and the defense of the island in times past. The Fortes trail starts in the village of Sao Sebastiao and takes you along the shoreline where you find the ruins of old Spanish forts, including the Fort of Santa Catarina, the Fort of Good Jesus, and the Greta Fort. These old forts, dating to the Spanish occupation in the 15th century, tell a story of intrigue, wars, fear, and the important role Terceira played in centuries past. You will also pass a lighthouse, an old watermill, numerous tidal swimming pools, and of course the shoreline lined with lava flows and basaltic rock. The contrast between sea and land will make for some beautiful sunsets for those into photography. The moderate linear trail is 5.7 km long, and the hike takes around three hours to complete.

Monte Brasil Hiking Trail

The hiking trail at Monte Brasil is a circular route that follows the outlying circle that leads around the entire volcanic cone and passes through the Castle or Fort of Sao Filipe. You will pass the war monument, the WWII embattlements, the Phoenician caves, and the parade ground between the two peaks. (Much more information on Monte Brasil will be discussed in this book under the section covering Angra do Heroismo). The hiking trail is 7.4km in length and some of the trail is on top of steep cliffs that fall directly into the sea. Caution should be taken during rainy weather when possible muddy areas may be present.

Castle of Sao Joao Baptista - Mount Brazil

Tourist Destinations

Angra do Heroismo City Gates

Angra do Heroismo

The UNESCO city of Angra do Heroismo has played a role in the development of the "New World" since the 15th century when in 1534 it was given city status. It is not just one city, but many cities in one, as the influences of each culture came and left their mark. They each added another stone to the cities' structure and construction. It was the city that many cities in Brazil are modeled after, and it became a pattern for urban development too. It is still the hub for commerce and tourism for Terceira today. It is the capital of Terceira, and the location of the main governmental offices, banks, commercial centers, supermarkets, historic landmarks, and other tourist destinations. Most hotels of Terceira have located here, as well as the "classy" restaurants of upscale tourism. It is a place of historical significance, as well as a place to explore architecture, churches, parks, and quaint sidewalk cafes. It is the center of all that happens on Terceira. It is the place of festivals and music venues. It hosts a movie theater and a bullfight ring. It is loaded with museums, local markets, cathedrals, libraries, and convents. It has the main hospital there on the outskirts of the town center, and the residential hospital can cater to the health care needs of tourists and locals alike. Around every corner, your senses will feel the vibe of this city, where new and old converge in a colorful mosaic of people and places to explore. So, come with me and let us begin to partake of this wonderful UNESCO city with all its activities.

Angra do Heroismo

- *Almeida Garrett Square* – The square in the center of the old town is adjacent to the Town Hall. It is a gathering place for light conversation and for families as they wait for the buses that regularly depart from here to other villages on the island. The post office is on the square, as well as small food vendors. A variety of shops line the square, and the 4-star hotel, "Azoris Angra Garden," faces the square with the rooms in the rear overlooking the Duke of Terceira Botanical Garden.

- *Duke of Terceira Gardens* – The Duke of Terceira Gardens located just off of the downtown square is filled with botanical jewels, many endemic just to Terceira and the Azores. It is well-manicured with plants from around the world, complete with walking paths, water features, a gazebo, and a terraced stair step leading to the Outeiro da Memoria, which is located on the hill, giving a panoramic view of the entire valley. The monument is a pyramidal structure sitting on the site of the original fort built in 1474 to protect the city from invasion. It was built to honor King Pedro IV's visit to Terceira. Winding your way back through the garden on your return to the town square, the quietness, the ambiance, and the rich aromas of flowering plants will engage your senses, and relax your soul. The municipal garden has no entrance fee and is a great place to spend time under a shady tree on a cool afternoon.

- *Convent of Sao Francisco* - The convent was the headquarters of the Franciscan Order of the Azores of Saint John the Evangelist. It was the first all-male monastery to be built in Angra but was closed when religious orders were banned in the 1800s. Paulo da Gama, the brother of Vasco da Gama, and Captain Vaz Corte Real are buried on site. It is also home to the "Church of our Lady of Guia." Today, it houses the Museum of Angra do Heroismo. This museum houses relics of the past as well as pieces reflecting geographical and technological innovations, along with children's toys and current items of interest.

- *Convent of Sao Concalo* – Today, the convent is just a shell of what was once a thriving colony of nuns under the Order of St. Clare. In 1832, all orders were banned from Terceira, thereby limiting the building's ability to house the historical relics of a time past. Today, you can admire the beautiful examples of Portuguese tile panels, baroque interior decorations, and intricate tapestries and canvasses. At one time, Angra housed nine convents.

- *Governor's Residence* – The building that stands today was once the home of the governor of Terceira, Joao Vaz Corte-Real, who in 1474, had his residence built here. Much of the original structure is still intact. It was placed in a strategic place at the foot of the caste for protection and security, and from there you can get a picture of the original beginnings of Angra.

- *Misericordia Church* – The church is located at the gates of the city. As you arrive from the harbor you will notice the two gates leading up to Angra by way of the Rua Direita, the beautiful cobblestone street that connects the wharf to the center square. At the entrance of the city there sits the beautiful Misericordia (Charitable) Church with its double bell towers and its blue and white façade. It greets all visitors to the city, and in the name of our Lord Jesus, it welcomes you. The church is the site of the first hospital built in the Azores. Inside it has beautiful opposing altars: the Altar of the Holy Spirit on the right and the Altar of the Holy Mercy of Christ on the left. The church is always a welcoming door for quiet prayer and meditation.

- *Conceicao Church* – The church was established on the site of an earlier hermitage. It was reconstructed in 1533 and is a fine example of renaissance style from the Baroque era. Its distinct style has been replicated across the island and is a classic example of Terceira's architectural heritage.

- *Santissmo Salvador da Se Church* – The church that stands today in renaissance splendor began in 1570. It is unique, in that, contrary to Portuguese church tradition, instead of facing Jerusalem, the church faces north. It is home to a beautiful, handcrafted altar made of Jacaranda (Brazilian wood) and whale ivory constructed in the Azores at the zenith of its importance. Also present are various silver religious artifacts that indicate the breadth and finesse of silversmithing in the Azores.

- *Caste of Sao Filipe and the Fort of S. Joao Baptista* – In an overpowering edifice of power, the castle or fort, the largest built by Spain in the entire Atlantic, sits overlooking the harbor as the guardian of peace for Angra. Built in 1592 at the request of Filipe II of Spain, the castle site of prominence completely covers all of Monte Brasil. It has controlled and protected the harbor from pirates, the English, and other opposing forces for almost five hundred years. The fort housed fifteen hundred soldiers in the 1500s and today is still used by the Portuguese Armed Forces. It has 4km of outer walls, four hundred pieces of historic artillery pieces, three square km of surface area, and is the oldest fort of Portugal that has been continually occupied. You will see the Spanish influence as well as the Portuguese in its architecture and historical significance. Inside the fort are a forest reserve, a children's park, a small zoo, and a hiking path. Some of the military areas are off-limits, but most of the castle can be explored without cost. [34]

---

[34] Angra do Heroismo, Terceira Tourist Office, Retrieved from

- *Se Street* – Se street is the commercial district of Angra, and many shops catering to both tourists and locals alike can be found there.

- *The University of the Azores* – Angra is also home to the only university on Terceira with an emphasis on the study of marine life and vulcanology.

- *Fort of Sao Sebastion* – On the other side of Angra harbor sits another fort that has been restored and is now a hotel and restaurant. As a guest, you can stay in one of the many rooms that were once important in the defense of the island but now are limited in use for tourists. There is a swimming pool on-site and a great overlook across the Atlantic where one can watch porpoises and whales play. You can catch a beautiful sunset from your deck chair as the sun descends into the ocean. The architect of the fort was an Italian native, and therefore, the fort has an Italian feel as to its construction.

Praia da Vitoria

www.visit.azores.com.

Praia da Vitoria is the second-largest city on Terceira. It is the city closest to the International Airport and Lajes Air Base, and therefore, plays an important role in the life of Terceira. It has a beautiful beach and marina and is an anchorage for yachts and a mooring for sea commerce. Even though the city is smaller than Angra, there is a variety of eating establishments and restaurants, including local cuisine, Chinese entrees, bakeries, fast food, sandwich shops, and ice cream parlors. There is a beautiful old town of about five blocks square that includes quaint whitewashed houses accented in bright colors and painted doorways. The main street, the Street of Jesus, is a patterned mosaic of cobblestones that end at the seashore roundabout. It is a pedestrian way that makes for easy strolling with your family and friends. Along the seafront are restaurants, cafes, and tourist shops, selling beachwear and trinkets. The beach itself is one of the few sandy beaches on the island. As the island is volcanic in origin, most of the swimming areas are surrounded by lava flows and black soil, however, Victory Beach of Praia is of pale-colored sand which is not found in most villages along the oceanfront. There are resort hotels in town, and the town is connected with a good bus service to Angra and other villages on the north side of the island. The airport is only ten minutes away from the town center, so Praia is a great place to relax before heading back to the airport.

Historical and Traditional Attractions

Bull Running and Bull Fights

In Praia da Vitoria, there is the local bull running that is traditionally known to be native to the island of Terceira only. Sometimes the bull is running after you and sometimes you are running after the bull, and sometimes everyone is just running for their lives. If by chance you happen to be here during their bull-running festivals, you can even run after the bull on the streets, in the square, and on the beach. If you choose to run on the beach, you had better be fast as there is no place to hide except to take to the water for protection.

Bull running is a local tradition that dates back to medieval times. The bull has a rope around its neck and then is released to chase mostly young men through the streets of the village. If the bull happens to get too involved or dangerous then there are a group of men in white shirts and black hats that are commissioned to take hold of the rope and drag you and the bull to safety. When asked what the point of the whole race or fight, or run, or whatever you call it, is for, the answer seemed to be that it is just a time for the young men to "show off" their manhood against a bull five times their size. The bull fight's purpose, unlike those in Iberia, is not to kill the bull, but just to have a social event where some chase the bull, some watch, and the six "pastores" direct the bull through the use of the cord that is attached to the bull's neck. It is from this cord that the fight gets its name, "tourada a corda." There is bullfight mania in the summer as a bullfight occurs almost every weekend in one of the villages across the island. Tourists are not encouraged to take part in the bull runs, but many do despite the warnings. However, it is a time for you as a tourist to participate, if only in sight, in an authentic tradition dating back over four hundred years. Similar runnings of the bull are seen in other places, but the use of the cord is only found in antiquity on the island of Grecian island of Crete. Who knows, maybe there is a connection after all to the "Phoenician" caves and their cultural relics discovered on Terceira.

There is a traditional Portuguese-style bull ring in Angra directly in front of the Three Bulls Monument. This stadium, "Praca de Toiros," appears to be like the bull rings found all over the Iberian peninsula, however, in Terceira, the way the bullfight is acted out is much different. This is an equestrian event with the matadors on horseback showing their skills against the bull but without the killing of the bull. They are dressed in the traditional colorful costumes for bullfighting and many matadors come from the mainland to host the fight. In the end, though, a group of men from Terceira, again in traditional costumes, will arrive to subdue the bull and bring him to his knees, albeit, without the killing of the bull. The crowd as in most events is loud, rowdy, and mainly men, who will cheer on the bullfighter at times, and at other times will cheer on the bull. I know it may not be your idea of the humane treatment of animals, but traditions die hard, and the traditional bullfight dates back to the beginning of time. Some say that the American cowboy and the South American gauchos are just an extension of the legacy of bullfighting and horsemanship. It is well if you put down your prejudices and come and watch.

Bull Running on Victory Beach

Allan Rodney Tilley

Bull Running on the Village Streets

Dairy Cows of Terceira

This would not be a tourist book if it failed to mention the black and white dairy cows of Terceira. They are picture-perfect for representing a relaxing scene of pure tranquility. Scattered across the island, whether on a mountain hillside or in a lowland pasture, there are cows, hundreds of cows. Drive down the back roads of the island and you will certainly meet cows in the middle of the road, being transferred from pasture to greener pastures. Every tourist that I have ever seen will have at least one picture of an Azorean cow in their portfolio. This abundance of cows lends itself to the production of a variety of milk and dairy products, including cheese making, yogurts, and ice cream. In every town, ice cream stands are a standard fare to be seen and experienced. It is something that if you could take home to all your neighbors in memory of your trip to Terceira, you definitely would. It is so fresh and natural, nothing can compare.

*One note – When driving make sure you understand that by law, cows in Terceira have the right of way. Yield always to the cows and please do not hit or injure one.

As the dairy industry is so much a part of the Terceira adventure, farm tours are available at various locations throughout the island. They will teach you and your children how to milk the cows, how to care for baby calves, and how to process the milk. You can also take a cheese lovers tour, which will take you for a behind-the-scenes look at a cheese factory, as you assist the cheesemakers in the entire process from milking to cheese fermentation. You will be able to sample cheese from Terceira of various ages and types and purchase cheeses of your choosing.

Connected with the dairy industry are the individual farms specializing in fruit and vegetable production. You can walk through a banana plantation, and fruit orchards, and sample fresh fruit that takes like natural pesticide-free nectar from the past, long before the processing begins so that the taste is not lost.

Native Lore and Handicrafts

Lace and Embroidery

In the past, Terceira had many native handicrafts including stone cutting, woodworking, masonry, and wall building. All of these can still be seen today, but they are a part of the natural daily routine of Terceira and the locals do not see these as handicrafts in the classic sense. They still make wine and cheese. They still repair the rock walls enclosing the pastures for cattle and sheep using local stone, and they still construct and repair age-old structures in much the same way they did for centuries.

However, for the tourist, it appears that folklore and handicrafts have not always been alive in their home countries, and for many of the handicrafts rightly so. Take, for instance, the making of lace. When the Flemish first came to Terceira and colonized the island in the 1400s, lace making was one of the skills the Flemish women brought with them, and it has continued to this day. In fact, lace and embroidery are still being stitched, and they are exported to the USA, Canada, Brazil, England, and Germany. In 1998, the making of lace was given a certificate of artisan and was recognized by the government of Portugal. There are factories on the island that can be toured to see the process of lace-making still being practiced today.

Pottery and Ceramics

Another popular artistic expression is the making of pottery and tiles. You may have noticed the popular blue artistic ceramic tile that gives each house its name and number. The street signs and notices are equally stylized. The particular azure blue-colored tiles are native to the Portuguese people. As the "Union Jack" is a symbol of England, Portuguese blue and white tiles are endemic to Portugal. You will see them in the museums, on the street corners, and as mosaics in homes and businesses. It is something that you will want to purchase to show an authentic craft from Terceira.

There are other private pottery shops or factories throughout the island with designs and patterns specific to the area. Pottery is also exported throughout Europe and the Americas and is one of the mainstays of the economy.

Silver making

Not as popular a craft as it once was, silver and jewelry making is still practiced locally but in limited quantities. You will see some exceptionally fine examples of this lost art in the various church's religious artifacts and in the city museums.

Chapter Four
Traditional Food of Terceira:

Alcatra

If there is one food that defines Terceira and the Azores, it is the traditional Portuguese pot roast which is known as "Alcatra." There is a legend that accompanies this Portuguese delicacy:

It appears that in the early settlement of Terceira in the 1400s that the original "Holy Ghost Festival" began after a series of violent earthquakes and volcanic eruptions. The people of the Azores were plagued by drought, crop failures, famine, and hunger. They were desperate for food, or for anybody that would alleviate the conditions, that if not corrected would ultimately lead them to starvation and death. They gathered together and prayed to the Holy Spirit for help. On the morning of Pentecost Sunday, at the rising of the sun, the settlers saw a ship on the horizon, and that ship was filled with food and the other necessities of life to sustain them. They shared the food with all the islanders, and they were saved. This started a tradition that has continued to this day known as the "Holy Ghost Festival." It is a time to feed the poor and share with others the stew and bread that is common to the Azores. It is a great time for communal meals shared with family and strangers alike.

All of Portugal, not just Terceira, celebrates this festival and it is connected to Queen Elizabeth (not of Britain) of Portugal, who upon hearing of this providence of God toward the people of the Azores, organized a holy processional in honor of the Holy Spirit. The queen's matrons carried the queen's crown through the streets of Lisbon to the city's cathedral where it was left on the altar. She then proceeded to give honor to the Holy Spirit in an act of thanksgiving. This commemorative event is still celebrated today with festivals across Portugal and the island of Terceira as well.

Alcatra is a meal slowed cooked in an earthenware large pot, not unlike the pots you see in the front yards of houses in which flowers are planted. However, today it is usually cooked in a slow crockpot cooker. It is a simple dish, but loved by all, and served in Portuguese restaurants around the world.

The Recipe for Alcatra is:

Ingredients:

- ½ lb. (1/4 kg.) of bacon, cut into small pieces
- 1 large onion, diced
- 2 bay leaves
- 1 tablespoon allspice berries
- ¼ teaspoon ground cinnamon
- 5 whole cloves
- 16 whole black peppercorns
- 4 garlic cloves, minced
- 2 tablespoons tomato paste
- 2 teaspoons salt
- 1 teaspoon ground black pepper
- 5 lb. (2kg) chuck roast, or rump roast
- 2 cups of red wine
- 2 cups water or beef stock

Cooking Instructions:

In a frying pan, fry bacon until just crisp over medium-high heat. Remove and allow to drain. Remove all but a small amount of bacon fat. Then add the onions, bay leaves, allspice, cinnamon, cloves, peppercorns, garlic, and tomato paste. Cook the onions until they are soft and clear, which is about 8-10 minutes. Remove the onion mixture to your slow cooker or earthen pot.

In a small glass bowl, mix the salt and pepper and spread the chuck or rump roast evenly. Sear the roast on each side in the hot stockpot. When all sides have been browned, place the roast on top of the onion mix in the slow cooker or pot.

Turn the heat up to high and add the wine and water and scrape up all of the browned bits on the bottom of the stockpot. Allow the wine mixture to boil for 5 minutes, and top with the bacon. Add more water, if necessary, to cover the roast. Cover and set the slow cooker for 8 hours (depending on the pot and cooker). At the four-hour mark, flip the roast over, cover, and continue to cook.

Serve with bread, rice, or vegetables and you are ready for your family meal. [35] [36]

Seafood

There can be no real reference to traditional dishes without the mention of seafood and the variety of meals connected to the sea. Fresh seafood, caught this morning and served the same day is a normal activity of life on Terceira. Fish is eaten that is boiled, fried, stuffed, minced, and the list of your desires can go on. All this and more can be found in every seafront village café. One of the most unusual dishes for most tourists, however, is the cooking of barnacles. In most countries, barnacles are not considered to be part of the menu. We indulge in oysters, shellfish, shrimp, fish, octopus, and the like, but barnacles are a rare treat. Personally, I have never eaten any, but I was told they are something that must be tried at least once.

---

[35] Alcatra – Portuguese Pot Roast in the Slow Cooker, Retrieved 2/10/2022 from http://farmgirlgourmet.com.
[36] Alcatra. Retrieved 2/10/22 from http://portugueserecipes.ca.com.

In addition to focusing on just the national dish or the unusual cuisine, you should focus on the plurality of cafes and restaurants that cater to your every need. Across the island, there are sandwich shops, Chinese restaurants, American hamburgers outlets, donut shops, and bakeries. In the main towns, you will find wholesome, filling meals to include vegetarian catered meals and meals made fresh from only locally supplied meats and vegetables. In truth, if Terceira were to be cut off from the mainland, they could be self-sufficient in their food production and survive indefinitely.

But you must not forget to indulge your passions in the great deserts that are available all across the island, whether it be the cakes and jams for an afternoon tea or the ice cream crepe that is eaten just before bedtime. In every small village, fresh-baked bread with accompanying smells will awaken your every sense. Take that first bite of bread, with a freshly brewed espresso, and you are ready for the day.

Since Terceira and Portugal are part of the European Union, you will find in the supermarkets and local shops your international favorites as well. Nothing is needed more as you go from café to your hotel room complete with your English toffees, your Belgian chocolates, and your best Azorean tea grown locally on the Island of San Miquel.

If you desire a lighter selection, pineapples and bananas, grown locally in the Azores, are at your fingertips, as well as a host of local fresh fruits and vegetables.

I guarantee though, that even with a light lunch and a hot coffee you will still go home a few pounds (kilos) heavier.

Chapter Five
Flora and Fauna:

Flora

If you desire an environmentally friendly green island that is almost untouched, then Terceira is your island. Per square acre, Terceira has more forest than the other islands of the Azores. Because of its climate, it is like a natural greenhouse in the middle of the Atlantic. Its forests are rich in Japanese Red Cedars, Azores Juniper, Cape Myrtle, Laurel, Whitewood, and over sixty various plant species unique only to the Azores. As you walk through the forests other species introduced into the island are also visible such as the eucalyptus trees and wild cedars, lending to a symphony of smells. There is nothing quite like the experience when the smell of the watery mist rises from the forest floor and mixes with the pollen wafting from the trees. You put that together with the natural heather, and it will cause your senses to come alive. You will spend hours in that special place taking it all in with all five senses.

Then there are the flowers. Since Terceira has a subtropical climate, flowers from around the world have been introduced, making Terceira a mosaic of all things blooming. The most prolific and famous of all flowers is the lilac hydrangeas that appear to cover the island. This "ball of thread" is found on every corner, lining the waterways, and highways, and filling the island with incredible beauty. The azaleas are equally intense and impressive, although not so prolific. You find them along the edges of crater lakes deep within the forests, and along busy urban streets as well.

The people of Terceira love their flowers and the vegetation constitutes a wall of color around the front and back gardens of most houses. Even as you enter the local homes, you will find pots of ivy hanging in the kitchen, and a plant or two adding that decorative touch throughout the house. And if you cannot find a special flower to your liking, then the municipal parks will be overflowing with new species set in a decorative mix that will surely catch your eye.

For many years during the early colonization of Terceira, the island was in a transition from a forest and woodland motif to a pastoral setting complete with miles of walled rock walls. With the advent of major tourism and the loss of traditional employment through whaling and fishing, the economy became to be centered around dairy production and tourism. They have found that the two entities can coexist in equal areas of significance, with each adding to the mix with commerce and environmentally green initiatives side by side in a sustainable stable economy.

Since the formulation of nature preserves and protected areas in the 1970s, it is sure that the forests and gardens of Terceira will bring pleasure to tourists for years to come, as well as enable valuable resources to be utilized in a sustainable environment.

Fauna

- Mammals: One thing that Terceira can be thankful for, is that when it comes to fauna, there are no snakes on the island. At the time of the discovery of Terceira in the 1400s, there were no terrestrial animals known to have existed on the island. However, two animals were in existence, but unknown in the 1400s, and that was the house mouse and a species of bat. In fact, in a recent study of the house mouse on Terceira, it was found that a species of mouse with particular DNA markers suggest that these house mice came to the island almost seven hundred years earlier than was previously thought. Some have suggested that Vikings may have visited the island when they were blown off course during one of their oceanic voyages. We know of no known Viking settlement and the archaeological studies appear to agree with that assumption. For all we know, the small house mouse may have arrived on Terceira through a random piece of flotsam.

- Birdlife: There is and has always been a wide variety of birdlife on the island. Seagulls abound as well as the most prevalent species, the tiny sparrow. Terceira lies between the West Atlantic and the East Atlantic flyways, and therefore it has one of the most diverse bird populations in the world. There are approximately 380 species of birds seen on Terceira, with only about twenty species that are there all year round. Many migratory birds are present throughout the year, and about fourteen species nest in Terceira in the summer. The only bird that is native to the islands is the Azorean Bullfinch. It does not live on Terceira, but only on the island of San Miguel. It is the second rarest bird in the world with only 775 individual birds still left on the island. Due to the deforestation of many of the islands, the bullfinch exists only in the area now declared a Special Protection Area on the eastern edge of the island of San Miquel.

On Terceira, there are four main habitat types and the birds you might see there:

- Marine – Yellow-legged Gull, Storm Petrel. Cory's Shearwaters, Common Tern
- Forest – God Crest, Chaffinch, Woodpigeon, Eurasian Blackcap
- Bodies of Water – Moorhen, Eurasian Coot, Grey Egret, Eurasian Teal, Eurasian Wigeon

- Pastures – Azores Quail, Island Canary, Common Snipe, Common Buzzard, Sparrow [37]

Birds have played a big part in the history of Terceira since it was the seagulls and their flight patterns that led the early explorers to continue on their oceanic voyages and to finally discover Terceira.

- Sea and Marine Life: The sea and Terceira have been intricately tied together since the beginning of time. Even before written history, Terceira's waters were teeming with fish. Because the Azores islands are the only islands located in such a strategic place in the North Atlantic, and valuable nutrients flow to the sea from the islands themselves, sea life has called Terceira home for centuries. Sitting on your balcony in your hotel room, you will see dolphins, porpoises, whales, and other marine life frolicking in the sea. You will see the waterspout from the blowhole of the larger whales, and if you are lucky, an upturned fin will emerge from the ocean depths as the massive whale plunges once again into the sea.

    Fish of every color, from the tiny pink and blue iridescent perch to the lowly bottom feeders, find their home in the waters surrounding Terceira. Sports fish such as tuna and the swordfish, and even random sharks find a way to add color and adventure to the sea. Because of the unpolluted waters, mollusks, crustaceans, octopuses, and barnacles attach to the rocks along the shallow waters and find their way to the plate of the fisherman and tourists alike. Other fish such as the Spanish mackerel will be caught, dried, and salted, later to be eaten by even the poorest of people on the island. It appears that Terceira is a natural warehouse of seafood just waiting to be sampled. Add also, the interior lakes and streams, filled

---

[37] *Azores Field Guide*, retrieved 2/10/2020 from http://eesc.columbia.edu.

with freshwater fish such as carp and perch, and even the newly introduced trout and you have a mouthful of delicacies.

- Insect life – Most tourists will probably not be interested to know about the myriad of insects living on the island. However, new species of insects are being discovered yearly as various insects from abroad arrive aboard planes, yachts, and floating debris. As of yet, no poisonous insects are known to exist on Terceira, and hopefully, that will continue for years to come. There are, however, some incredibly unique species of insects that have been discovered in the vast volcanic cave system that is spread under the island. Some of these insects have yet to be named or even identified.

Chapter Six
People and Culture:

Local Traditions

As soon as you arrive in Terceira, you will notice that there is not a homogeneous, one size fits all, type of person who you would call an Azorean. You will see a person olive in complexion next to a red-haired child with blue eyes. There is a kind of Mediterranean look, but one that is definitely a unique combination of all nationalities that have passed through the island. First, there was the Flemish from Northern Europe, followed by those from the Iberian Peninsula. Later slaves who worked the fields early in the life of the island, mixed with Moors and Jews and would add to the blend of cultures and ethnicity. Recently after much immigration, especially after WWII, even the American soldiers would add to the mix. This blended society emerged as a certain typical islander that is relaxed, who enjoys life, and is friendly with everyone. Since the population is relatively small, everybody knows each family by name, and from what village your ancestry resides. At times, the locals can be clannish since there are some local language dialects that designate whether one is from the north or the south. It seems that on a small island this would not be possible, but in the past, if villagers were separated by merely twenty miles, it would be a long bridge to cross linguistically.

But in recent years, the culture is changing, as the population has been on the move literally. In the 2001 census, the population of the Azores was 242,073 inhabitants, almost the same as it was one hundred and fifty years ago. After a series of volcanic eruptions, economic hardships, war, and political upheaval, the population began shifting. With this move and the migration to the Americas, the people of Terceira were no longer an isolated, indigenous population. The mixing of cultures has altered the "culture" that defined the people of Terceira. There are still many traditions firmly held, as seen in the numerous festivals that occur across the island, but the one uniting element for Terceira is the Catholic religion. Most of the festivals are linked to religious holidays. This does make a united force as people come together to eat together, play together, and also pray together. There are pilgrimages, holy places, acts of piety, and religious devotion held by many people across the island. Terceira is known as the island of festivals, or as some say, "the party island." But "party" in Terceira is not translated as in most other western countries, for it does not translate into a vibrant nightlife. No, a party in Terceira is usually linked to a religious family festival, a bullfight, a soccer game, or a day at the beach. It is just more calming and peaceful, with a strong connection to the outdoors. Tourists who come to Terceira looking for a gaudy beach romp will be sorely disappointed.

Imperios Holy Spirit Chapel

You can also see this link to the religious past as you notice that each village has a shrine to the "Holy Spirit." These small colorful little chapels called "Imperios" (Empires) are neighborhood centers for the Festival of the Holy Spirit. The festivals will be held across the island villagers during the summer months and into the fall. The event will last a week, beginning with a parade through the village streets by the locals in their native costumes. This is followed by music, fireworks, food, and fun. It is a time to honor God through acts of service, such as in the feeding of the poor and helping your neighbor. In each village, a committee will select a village household where all week that family will function as a chef, feeding all those that come to their home. It is an extreme honor to be chosen as the host, and the neighbors pitch in baking bread and preparing food. The Imperios (Imperial) or chapel is the center point where the Holy Spirit is honored, and God is given thanks for the favor and blessings the village felt. If you happen to be traveling through one of these villages during the festival, a local villager may stop you and give you freshly baked bread as a sign of friendship and a sign of God's generosity to all. Terceira is the main island for the Imperios tradition, and it brings the island into one homogeneous family, linked to religious belief and practice.

The culture is also linked to the sea. On days off of work, you will find the men lining the breaker walls and on top of the rocks fishing and enjoying the company of friends as well as partaking in the peace of God's creation.

It seems you could boil the culture down to family, faith, and friendship. That formula has been the foundation for the peace and safety one feels when visiting the island. It just feels right.

Religious Life

From the beginning of Portugal's exploration and colonization, the Catholic Church played a significant role in the culture of Terceira's development. The church and the state were many times one and the same, and Portugal's conquests were driven by both commerce and religious fervor. Because of the commandment in the Bible to go out into all the world and preach the gospel (Matthew 28:19), the Catholic Church of Portugal had a priority to seek to settle and to convert those people to which they encountered. They not only built churches, but they built hospitals, schools, universities, and charity organizations. The church was immensely powerful and influential in all the affairs of culture and government. Some of that influence was lost when religious orders were banned in Terceira, but the people have carried the church and faith in their hearts for generations. A majority of the island is of the Catholic faith at this time and although attendance at the local parish church is not as significant as in times past, there still is a strong religious adherence. The times for Catholic Mass and the service times for other church activities are listed on the various church websites, the church bulletin boards, and in their informational brochures. There are no services available in languages other than Portuguese in the Catholic churches, however, if religious help is needed, many of the priests speak English.

There are other faiths represented on the island as well. As recently as twenty years ago, Jewish religious life, through a small contingent of Jewish people, was still being observed on the island. Most of the Jewish population has immigrated in recent years, but they still left their mark on the island. Port Juneau, the Port of Jews, is named from an earlier time when Jews fled from the Iberian peninsula and the Spanish Inquisition of 1492 to seek freedom in Terceira. About 80,000 Jews crossed over from Spain to Portugal and some made their way to Terceira. [38] A Jewish cemetery is still in existence in Angra where many of the early Jewish settlers who came first to Terceira are buried.

Protestant churches are also present in Angra including the Evangelical Baptist Church, the New Apostolic Church, the Seventh Day Adventist Church, and the Assemblies of God Church. There is only one English-speaking church, the Azorean Baptist Church, which exists on the island, and it is located near Praia da Vitoria.

There is a Protestant cemetery in S. Bras which contains forty-two graves, most from WWII.

---

[38] Armstrong, K. (2000). *The Battle for God.*, New York, New York: Alfred A. Knoff Publishing.

Immigration

Despite an economic climb, many people from the Azores continue to migrate to other nations. Most immigration in recent years has been to America, Canada, and Brazil. In fact, there are more people from the Azores that reside permanently out of the Azores than in them. Most of the islands of the archipelago have lost population except for the islands of Terceira and San Miquel. Some have said that Terceira is the 51st state of America because so many people who are from Terceira live in either California or Massachusetts. The migration is not a recent event because for years there was a connection between the whalers from Nantucket, Massachusetts with those in the whaling industry on the Azores. Sailors and whalers from their native countries were looking for the same thing; whales, and since Terceira was in the middle of the Atlantic Ocean it was a perfect place to resupply and make repairs on the whaling vessels. Therefore, the link between New England and the Azores has been strong and stable. Even in the book by Herman Melville, "Moby Dick," he wrote, *"No small number of these whaling seamen belong to the Azores, where the outbound Nantucket whalers frequently touch to augment their crews from the hardy peasants of those rocky shores...How it is, there is no telling, but Islanders seem to make the best whalers."*[39]

However, there were other major migrations too such as those that happened after the catastrophic eruptions and earthquakes that have occurred since the occupation of the islands. Today in California it is claimed that, outside of the Azores, they have the highest concentration of islanders than any other place on earth. They came for jobs, for prosperity, and never returned home except for the summers when they would visit the grandparents they had left behind.

---

[39] Powers, J. (2021, November 4). The Azores. *The Inquirer and Mirror*.

The Azores are so linked to the history of Massachusetts that in Angra do Heroismo, there is a plaque that commemorates the city's sisterhood with the city of Taunton, Massachusetts. The plaque promotes the idea that over a century before the Pilgrims of England's arrival, someone from the Azores settled in Massachusetts. This fact is said to be based on the discovery of what has become to be known as, "Dighton Rock." This forty-ton boulder on the Taunton River has complex markings that seem to indicate that the Portuguese explorer, Miguel Corte Real, arrived in 1511 and lived among the indigenous Indians there. He seemingly left his mark, the Portuguese cross and the Portuguese coat of arms on the rock, now known as, "Dighton Rock." If this is indeed true, then the Portuguese, and not only Columbus, were in America long before it was recorded in history books. [40]

There was as well further immigration to the USA and Canada through the servicemen and women who resided at Lajes Air Force Base and intermarried with the locals.

Lately, immigration has leveled off, and on a few islands, there has been an increase in the population. With the advent of Portugal being included in the European Union and NATO, there has been a greater level of economic development and a growing ex-pat community. If you look at the new demographics, more people from America, Canada, and Northern Europe are moving to Terceira. If this continues, along with added amenities, better healthcare, and an openness to new arrivals, Terceira can curtail the bleed that is endangering the island's long-term recovery.

---

[40] Ibid

Chapter Seven
Art and Architecture:

They say that art is where you find it. If that is so, then the art displayed on the island of Terceira is first found in caves, dating to the Bronze Age [41] Although, from then until now, old medieval monasteries, Imperios, and churches that are seen scattered across the island are the source of art and religious relics from the 1500s on. As these works of art are not cataloged, it is a challenge for the tourist to find the origin of many of these pieces of art.

---

[41] Matos, C., Archaeology: Prehistoric rock art found in caves on Terceira Island – Azores. Retrieved 2/28/2022 from http://portuguese-american-journal.com/archaeology-prehistoric-rock-art-found in caves-on-terceira-island-azores/

Nonetheless, art and architecture are readily seen in the museums, and on the streets of Angra. It is seen in the beautiful mosaics set into the street cobblestones to the wrought iron window dressings and the red roof terracotta tiles. When you step onto the streets of Angra do Heriosmo you step back in time to an era of colonization and medieval architecture. You feel like Columbus could meet you at the corner café for a coffee and a croissant. It is incredible for the red roof tile houses combined with the bright colored trim on white-washed houses just burst with color as if a painting has just been drawn. In Angra, you have the Museum of Sacred Art on Rua da Rosa street which is filled with intricate silver works, native wood carvings, painted icons, and tiled mosaics.

However, you do not have to pay to see fine art as one can just step inside any of the churches or convents and be taken back to an age of religious dedication and service. Altars and tables of sacraments are gilded with gold and silver to display the grandeur that the conquest of the New World brought.

For example, take the Se Cathedral, located in Angra, with its splendor both inside and out that highlights baroque art in renaissance style. The present cathedral was built in the 16th century over the ruins of an earlier gothic church first built in the 1500s. The silver frontal of the Altar of the Blessed Sacrament built by Manuel Camerio between 1702-1720 is a beautiful masterpiece to behold. It continues to remind us of the piety and love for our Savior shown in the hands and minds of ordinary citizens. Additionally, the entire edifice both inside and out, shouts out praises to Christ our King. It causes one to enter a silence of reverent prayer as you enter the sanctuary.

Then there are the convents, one in particular, the Convent of S. Goncalo, that still retains many features of the old world. It has been remodeled and renovated over time, but much of the original building has remained intact. It still has two cloisters, monastic cells, kitchens, and dining rooms. Of special interest is the church nave with two overlapping choirs that are separated by a majestic Baroque gilded wood carving. There are the large oil paintings, silver inlay, Portuguese tile panes, historic religious sculptures, and the hand-carved pews noted for their magnificent figures. The convent is the oldest in the city and was under the auspices of the Order of Saint Claire. (Saint Claire is the female contemporary of Saint Francis) This convent was the only convent allowed to remain open after the expulsion of religious orders in 1832 by governmental decree. The last nun died in 1885 and the convent was closed. It remains in use today as a kindergarten. [42]

---

[42] Goncalves, C. *"Church and Convent of S. Goncalo"* in *"Discover Baroque Art,"* Museum With No Frontiers, 2022. Retrieved 2/26/2022 from http://baroqueat.museumwnf.org/database_item.php?id=monument;BAR;pt;Mon1 1;5;en.

Chapter Eight
Practical Tips for Tourists:

1. The proper greeting for meeting someone is to shake hands, even for little children.

2. If you are invited into a person's house, always remove your shoes and bring a small gift of appreciation. If offered a drink, take it with a heart of thankfulness.

3. When driving, the lanes are small and there is only one motorway on the island, so drive slowly.

4. Always remember to bring rain gear if going on a hike or outing as the weather changes almost instantly at times.

5. People are proud of Terceira, so don't compare it to the USA or Spain, or any other nation. Just compliment them on their island.

6. If you are a little late to an event, say 15 minutes or so, that is not too important as you want to give extra time to make sure your host is ready.

7. Learn a bit of Portuguese. It goes a long way to show interest in the islanders.

8. If you go somewhere special, dress up, not down.

9. If you enter a church, please show respect by whispering, or praying silently.

10. If you eat at a restaurant moderately priced and up, tipping is not mandatory but expected.

11. Listen first, then speak, and make sure you are not too boisterous or loud in your conversation.

12. Lastly, show respect to the islanders and the island, and do not litter.

Chapter Nine
Facts and Figures:

Terceira Tourist Office
Rua Direita, 74
9700-066 Angra do Heriosmo
Terceira, Azores, Portugal
Tel. +351-295-404-800
Email: dt.terceira@azores.gov.pt

EVT – Bus Timetables
Angra do Heriosmo
Rua Dr. Sousa Meneses, No. 15
9700-194 Angra do Heriosmo

Police/Policia
295-212-022

Emergency/Emergencia/SOS
112

Taxi
295-212-404 – Angra do Heriosmo
295-212-004 – Angra do Heriosmo
295-512-092 – Praia da Vitoria

Portugal Embassy in the United States
2012 Massachusetts Ave. NW
Washington D.C. 20036 USA
Tel. 202-350-5400

Portugal Embassy in Canada

645 Island Park Drive
Ottawa, Ontario K1Y 0B8 Canada
Tel. 613-729-0883

Portugal Embassy in Great Britain
11 Belgrave Square
London, SW1X 8PP
Tel. (44) 2072355331

Chapter Ten
Terceira Trivia:

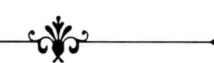

Questions:

1. What is the name of the people who lead the bulls around on a rope in the Terceira bullfight?

2. What are the small chapels that are dedicated to the Holy Spirit and are found scattered throughout the island of Terceira?

3. Why is the island now called Terceira?

4. What is the name of the cake that is traditional to the island and named after a queen?

5. What is the name of the traditional meat dish served throughout the island and steeped in legend?

6. What is the name of the type of bullfight found only on Terceira?

7. Where does the most important religious pilgrimage of Terceira start?

8. The Holy Spirit Festival is associated with what queen?

9. What is the name of the first official city on Terceira?

10. What was the name first given to the island of Terceira?

Answers:

1. The pastores which translated into English mean, shepherds.

2. The chapels are called Imperios or Empires.

3. The island was named Terceira or third as it was the third island of the Azores discovered by the Portuguese.

4. The queen's cake is called, "Dona Amelia."

5. The meat dish of pot roast, "Alacatra."

6. The bullfight is called the street cord fight due to the use of a rope to control the bull.

7. The pilgrimage starts at the village of Serreta.

8. The Holy Spirit Festival is associated with Santa Isabel (Queen Elizabeth).

9. The first city with official recognition is Angra do Heroismo.

10. Terceira was first named the "Island of Jesus Christ."

Attributions

All pictures in this book not listed below are the sole property of Sarah Harvey Tilley, photographer.

Pictures/Photographs:

Pp. vi - Rodrigo-Ramos-WVycxvFT_Km – Unsplash.com.

Pp. 1 - USGS- public domain.

Pp. 8 -Public domain photo by Vera Gorbunova on Unspash.com.

Pp. 14 -Cart ruts retrieved 1/20/22 Rodregues, F., Madruga, J., Martins, N. and Cardoso, F. (2018).

Dating the Cart-Ruts of Terceira Island, Azores, Portugal. *Archaeological Discovery*, 6,

279-299, DOI:10.4236/ad.2018.64014 retrieved 1/10/22 from

https://doi.org/10/4236/ad.2018.64014 and can be found also on research gate.com –public domain

Pp. 17 - OpenStreetMap, CC by _SA 3.0 http://creativecommons.org/licenses/by-sa/3.0/wiki.

Pp. 21 – St. Brenden – public domain.

Pp. 24 – Henry the Navigator – public domain.

Pp. 26 – Atlantis map- public domain.

Pp. 27 – Church – public domain.

Pp. 27 – Bruges- Wikimedia commons – public domain.

Pp. 29 – Columbus – Wikimedia commons – public domain.

Pp. 32 – Vasco da Gama – Bose d' Anjou from NY, NY USA CC by 2.0 via Wikimedia commons.

Pp. 40 - Lajes Airfield, Public Domain.

Pp. 46 – Terceira_Algar_do_Carvao_2 by Unokorno on Unsplash.com.

Pp. 50 – Fountain – public domain.

Pp. 58 – Fort- public domain.

Pp. 70 – Lace- antique-honiton-lace-gc8826a966_1920 – public domain – on pixabay.

Pp. 74 – Meat – public domain on pixabay.

Pp. 85 – Imperios – public domain on Wikimedia commons.

Pp. 90/Pp.912 – House and Se Cathedral – Jose' Luis Avila Silveria/Pedro Noronha e Costa – Public Domain as per Wiki Media Commons.

Logos on the front and back page courtesy of Microsoft Word.

Additional Books by Allan Rodney Tilley

A History and Guide to Biblical Sites in Cyprus

Communion with God and Community with Man

The 38 Days of Christmas Devotional

Biblical Hospitality: The Chain that Links Fellowship to Faith

Finding Christ in Muslim Lands

I Know Nothing and Other Lessons I Learned by being on the Mission Field

A History and Guide to Biblical Sites in Cyprus – Large Print Edition

***All books are available on Amazon.com or on your Kindle device.*

Made in the USA
Las Vegas, NV
24 June 2023